GOLDHAWK ROAD

WASTED

BAD COMPANY

Simon Bent

GOLDHAWK ROAD

WASTED

BAD COMPANY

OBERON BOOKS

LONDON

WWW.OBERONBOOKS.COM

First published in 1997 by Oberon Books Ltd
521 Caledonian Road, London N7 9RH
Tel: +44 (0) 20 7607 3637 / Fax: +44 (0) 20 7607 3629
e-mail: info@oberonbooks.com
www.oberonbooks.com

Reprinted in 2011

ISBN 978-1-87025-964-4

Cover design: Andrzej Klimowski

Printed by CPI Antony Rowe, Chippenham

CONTENTS

INTRODUCTION

Paul Miller

Like many writers, Simon keeps a notebook, and the frequency of its appearance out of his overcoat varies. Snapshots of incidents and overheard phrases are recorded with an often gleeful disregard of overt intention which might dismay the innocent observed.

This unfairly obtained (inadmissable?) evidence of course offers truer insights than more rational or judicious accounts would allow, and tends to pile up in the notebooks like a snowdrift. Reassembled into his characteristic jazzy, impressionistic mosaics, they form a texture at once bizarre and real. And, as Humphrey Bogart said of acting, if that sounds easy, try it.

There is a time delay in this process of accumulation, and in view of certain of the subjects which find echo in these plays it is just as well, though friends have noted a somewhat alarming acceleration recently. The coarse chuckle of private delight that accompanies the notebook's return to the overcoat pocket, some new treasure-trove safely stowed, betrays the happiness of someone briefly stealing a march on an otherwise uncompromising world.

Given this possibly furtive, if not actively sinister, portrait of an artist, it is fortunate that the outlook of Bent's work is ultimately benign. A side-effect of the Royal Court revolution was the imperative that young men be 'angry', as defined in increasingly narrow journalistic terms. (And not just by the press – theatres, too, continue to prescribe agendas. Today, violence is sexy.) The anger here at the casual waste of human possibility is vehement yet implicit (except in the titles – *Goldhawk Road* was originally *Damaged*). Paradoxically, what one experiences is also oddly celebratory, not at all misanthropic. For some reason it still surprises that Bent's writing produces such a breathtakingly delighted response in an audience, from dialogue which might appear on the page rather numinous to an over-literary mind.

Actors, of course, seize on it with a thirst. His writing has attracted a stunning array of actors, and the fondness is mutual – I've watched Simon be influenced by them all in ways too potent and subtle to go into here. The plays are not by any means easy to get right, but they certainly engender extraordinarily happy rehearsal periods.

Now is an exciting time to be in the theatre again. After the apparent dispersal of new writing in the eighties, when writers were squeezed out of the dialogue between critics and directors which characterised the period, young audiences have begun to return to see their lives represented.

Thanks to the seed-work of a few key theatres a new movement of writers with a strikingly independent tone and stance has come to prominence. The fact that our interest has returned to the writer is a sign of the health of this new cultural spurt of growth. It's no accident that all this is happening at the same moment as Britpop, and there is (though they will curse me for saying it) a similarly cocky wilfulness to the work of, say, Nick Grosso, Joe Penhall, Jez Butterworth and Martin McDonagh as well as films like *Boston Kickout* and *Trainspotting*. The press have even minted one of their more tiresome phrases ('laddism') in order to throw a blanket over it all, the 'new lad' thus joining his equally fictitious older friend the 'new man'.

What is new is that these writers and their work are being put at the centre of things. Eighties revivalism, the directorial signature writ large, is thankfully dying. If all this is to continue, though, directors in power will have to follow through on this groundwork. This means loyalty – the writer's next play may not be what you had in mind. An oasis of such loyalty was provided to this writer by Peter Gill at the National's Studio (and later by Dominic Dromgoole at the Bush). What I think we need slightly less of is the kind of 'script development' that the theatre has taken to apeing from the movies. At least when there's a camera involved there is usually some financial reward for all the hoops the 'scriptwriter' has to jump through.

The background to these three plays could hardly be more different, and yet the people in them share common tendencies which put them at odds with themselves, each other and the rest of the world. Loss predominates. They are missing fathers, missing sons, missing best-friends, boyfriends, pills and keys. "Where's everyone gone?". In short they have, of course, lost the plot. They substitute obsessions, fantasies of control and gratification that take many forms.

Reading the three plays together, I long to introduce the characters to each other. Would the restless young of *Bad Company* take comfort in the anxiously distressed lives of those in *Wasted*, or the rootless disunity of the *Goldhawk Road* crowd? Would they carry on putting up their petulant front to the world, their simple human needs barely concealed? Or, witnessing their depression blossoming in such exotic landscapes, would they be less inclined to dreams of escape?

London 1997

GOLDHAWK ROAD

Characters

MARY

JOHN

JO

PAUL

JULIA

COLIN

REG

RALPH

The plays is set in the present, London. The action takes place in the back room of an end of terrace Victorian worker's cottage.

The room is barely decorated and furnished; a large old imitation Persian rug that doesn't cover the whole floor, a table and chairs and an old sofa. Downstage left is the door to the hall and front door; this doorway also leads directly to the foot of the kitchen. Upstage left is the door to the cellar; the cellar has been converted into a bathroom and toilet. On the back wall, upstage left of the kitchen, is a window looking out onto the back yard and west facing. The downstage front wall would be wooden doors, stretching the width of the room, that when opened make the front room and back room into one large room. Upstairs is a large bedroom at the front of the house, (over the front room), a medium sized bedroom over the back room, and over the kitchen two small bedrooms.

Goldhawk Road was first performed at the Bush Theatre, on 5th January 1996, with the following cast:

MARY, Elizabeth Bell

JOHN, Jack Carr

JO, Suzanne Hitchmough

PAUL, Trevor Martin

JULIA, Julie Saunders

COLIN, John Simm

REG, Neil Stuke

RALPH, Danny Webb

DIRECTION: Paul Miller

DESIGN: Michael Taylor

LIGHTING DESIGN: Andy Phillips

MUSIC: Terry Davies

SOUND: Paul Bull

ACT ONE

Scene 1

PAUL asleep on the sofa. COLIN barefoot sorting out a pile of socks into pairs and throwing aside those with holes in them.

COLIN: No way man, there's no bloody way. Bollocks. You're ugly.

Enter REG with a bag of fish and chips.

REG: Don't say it right, I know what you're going to say, so don't. Don't.

Exit REG.

COLIN: She wouldn't have, not even if you begged her for it.

Enter REG.

REG: Where's the ketchup?

COLIN: You're late.

REG: Don't.

COLIN: Where have you been?

REG: I said don't, Colin. We haven't got any ketchup.

COLIN: I got barbecue sauce instead.

REG: What did you get barbecue sauce for, we haven't got a barbecue, when was the last time you went to a barbecue?

COLIN: I like barbecue sauce.

REG: And I like ketchup.

COLIN: You do the shopping then.

REG: I like ketchup.

COLIN: You're late.

REG: You've been taking drugs again – "There's blood on my

trousers Reg. I've murdered a baby Reg." I don't do the shopping.

COLIN: So what did he say?

REG: I'm eating my dinner, alright.

COLIN: Where's mine?

REG: You said you were going shopping.

COLIN: I did.

REG: So next time get some ketchup.

COLIN: Go on, give us a chip.

Silence. COLIN takes a chip, REG belts his hand.

Come on then.

REG: I'm having my dinner.

COLIN: Go on.

REG: You couldn't.

COLIN: Oh yeah?

REG: Yeah.

Have a chip brother.

Throws a chip at COLIN.

COLIN: You're not my bloody brother right, he's not my dad – my mam doesn't even know him. (*To PAUL.*) A sad lonely coach driver she once served egg and chips to.

REG: When did she serve him egg and chips?

COLIN: I don't know – she worked in a transport café, alright.

REG: Alright. Have a chip.

Colin doesn't take one.

So go home then.

COLIN: Yeah.

COLIN goes back to sorting socks.

REG: Ralph says we can have a cheque now or cash later, so I says we'll have cash, alright.

COLIN: I'm not having a cheque.

REG: He's gone to Redhill.

COLIN: I can't have a cheque, cheque's no good to me.

REG: You're not getting a cheque.

COLIN: He's your friend, tell him I don't want a cheque.

REG: Pack it in will you. Go on have a chip.

COLIN: He's hid my shoes. Where's Redhill?

REG: How the fuck should I know.

COLIN: I can't find my shoes.

REG: You're a mess. Look at you – get your hair cut, you need a haircut.

COLIN: What size feet are you?

REG: Eight.

COLIN: They don't look eight.

REG: Bugger off they're mine.

COLIN: He's hid my shoes.

> *COLIN lights a fag.*

I smoke, alright.

REG: Thought you were stopping.

COLIN: I did. They don't look eight.

REG: They're mine, alright. You've done too many drugs that's your problem.

COLIN: I don't do drugs any more, right.

REG: Right. What about them?

COLIN: I need these for my health... they keep me... if I don't have a... it's like being in space without an oxygen pipe. What's Ralph gone to Redhill for?

REG: To see a fat bloke called Vincent about getting us our money.

COLIN: Vincent?

REG: Yeah.

COLIN: Vincent?

REG: Have you fed him yet?

COLIN: He's hid my shoes, let him get his own bloody dinner.

REG: Alright Colin, steady on.

COLIN: Where's Redhill?

REG: How should I know.

COLIN: What?

REG: Nothing.

COLIN: No what?

REG: Nothing.

COLIN: Come on, out with it.

PAUL turns in his sleep.

PAUL: Mary.

REG: (*Together.*) Fuck off.

COLIN: (*Together.*) Fuck off.

Enter JOHN. Dirty hands and face.

REG: Oh aye, it's the King.

JOHN: He's still asleep then.

COLIN: Yeah, that's what he does.

Exit JOHN.

REG: We'll get paid, alright – he's never not paid before has he – he's always late, he wouldn't be Ralph if he wasn't late paying. Right.

COLIN: Right.

REG: He's not worth it.

COLIN: Right.

REG: So make some tea.

COLIN: Right. Yeah but –

REG: Stop it right.

COLIN: Right. But what if –

REG: He'll pay.

COLIN: But what if he doesn't?

REG: He'll pay.

COLIN: But what if he doesn't?

REG: I'll go round and kill him, right.

COLIN: Right. I'll come with you.

REG: Yeah.

COLIN: Yeah. But he's your friend.

REG: Yeah.

COLIN: Yeah.

REG: It's not worth the bother, he's not worth it, Ralph's not worth it, fat Vincent, nothing's worth it.

COLIN: I know that, you think I don't know nobody's worth it?

REG: Alright. Look, why don't you –

COLIN: What – what – why don't I what? My mam never did, she never, not with him.

REG: You've got his nose.

COLIN: No I haven't, this is my nose, my nose is nothing like his nose – you've got his nose.

REG: So I get all his money.

COLIN: He's hid my shoes. Where have you hid my shoes...

I'll kick you – I bloody will...

REG: He's asleep.

COLIN: He's not asleep.

REG: Leave him alone.

Enter JOHN cleaned up.

How's your bus?

JOHN: I'll take him for a spin round the M25 when he wakes up.

REG: Your bus all clean is it?

JOHN: It's not a bus, it's a coach.

COLIN: It looks like a giant blue cock on wheels, with go faster stripes down the side of it.

REG: Yeah, nice bus.

JOHN: It's a coach a Volvo coach.

COLIN: A Volvo.

JOHN: Yes.

COLIN: From Sweden.

REG: You want to make sure it's locked up properly at night.

JOHN: You touch my coach son and I'll use your head to clean out the toilet with.

REG: Oh yeah?

JOHN: Yeah. It's lucky for you I'm a guest of your dad's.

COLIN: He's not my dad.

REG: Both my parents are dead.

JOHN: Oh, I see. So what are you doing here then?

REG: We're looking after him, he's a sick old man. He wrote my mother a letter –

COLIN: And mine.

REG: Only my mam's dead so I had to open it; in it he says he's sorry he hasn't been in touch for nearly thirty years, but now he's dying and as he's my dad can I come and see him and make up for lost time.

COLIN: Yeah.

REG: Which was funny at the time, as I thought I'd buried my dad only three years before, he died of cancer like my mam.

JOHN: Oh, I'm sorry.

REG: Why, you didn't know them did you?

JOHN: No. It must have come as a bit of a blow to to find out your dad was still alive.

REG: No not really, I'd always had my suspicions. Then I met him.

COLIN: He promised to remember us in his will if we stayed and looked after him – he said he was dying.

JOHN: So how long have you been here?

REG: Just over a year.

COLIN: Six months – his letter got lost in the post.

REG: How long are you visiting for?

JOHN: Oh, I don't know – I'm on holiday.

COLIN: Have you shagged the cleaning lady yet?

JOHN: Don't talk about Mary like that.

COLIN: Like what?

JOHN: Watch your mouth you. She looks after him.

REG: Why don't you go and drive your bus.

JOHN: I'm warning you.

COLIN: He's on holiday. Do you always take your coach on holiday with you. What's wrong with your wife?

REG: Looks like the back end of a bus.

COLIN: She doesn't go as well as his coach.

JOHN: Just watch it right, I was in the merchant navy for five years.

Enter MARY with shopping.

MARY: It's not safe, the streets aren't safe, there's a coloured gentleman singing and dancing on the corner.

JOHN: Oh, Mary.

MARY: I had to cross the road.

JOHN: It's frightening.

MARY: An old man carrying on in the street like that.

JOHN: They like to drink.

MARY: He wasn't drunk.

REG screws up his fish and chips.

COLIN: What d'you do that for?

MARY: He lunged at me and asked to carry my bags.

REG throws screwed up chips on floor.

COLIN: Ah, what.

JOHN: It's outrageous.

MARY: I had to cross the road.

JOHN: It's London Transport I blame.

COLIN: I can't eat those now.

REG: Bloody hell.

JOHN: Mind your language you.

COLIN: Look at them.

PAUL: Mary.

MARY: The streets aren't safe.

JOHN: Where do you want these bags putting?

PAUL: Mary – is that you Mary?

MARY: Oh, don't trouble yourself.

JOHN: Nothing's too much for you Mary.

MARY: I'll be alright, I can manage – I'll manage them in the kitchen myself.

PAUL: My arm, oh my arm – I had a dream, a terrible frightening dream, it was dark, I was alone and there was nobody and then I woke up and... who are you?

JOHN: It's me John.

PAUL: John.

JOHN: You know Johnny.

PAUL: I'm fat.

MARY: I'll put them in the kitchen myself then.

COLIN: Yeah.

MARY: You carry on, don't mind me.

PAUL: Mary.

JOHN picks up the bags.

JOHN: I'll put them in the kitchen.

PAUL: Somebody do my arm will you.

JOHN: We could go for a drink later if you like.

MARY: I don't drink.

JOHN: You could have a Babycham.

PAUL: I'm dying.

JOHN: In the kitchen then.

PAUL: Somebody help me.

JOHN: Anything for you Mary.

MARY: How much longer are you staying for?

JOHN: Oh, just a couple more days I should think.

Exit JOHN.

PAUL: I'm dying.

MARY: You're not dying. I'll put the receipt on the side, you
can settle up with me at the end of the week.

PAUL: I'm dying.

MARY: You're not dying.

COLIN: Let him die if he wants.

MARY clips COLIN around the ear.

All I said was –

MARY: He's your father.

COLIN: I'll talk to him how I want then.

MARY: After all he's done for you.

COLIN: What's he done for me – I didn't even know he was my dad until six months ago.

MARY: The ingratitude. If it wasn't for him you wouldn't be here.

REG: Yeah, you were conceived on the back seat of his coach outside a transport café, him and your mam.

COLIN: No, she never.

REG: On the same back seat as he did it with with my mam.

PAUL: Mary.

MARY: Oh shut up will you.

REG: Now look at him.

COLIN: He's not my dad.

PAUL: Somebody help me.

REG: You spoil him.

Exit REG.

COLIN: He's hid my shoes.

Exit COLIN with socks. MARY picks up the chips.

PAUL: I'm dying.

Enter JOHN with a can of beans.

JOHN: Where does he keep his beans.

MARY takes the beans.

We could go for a drive later, if you like – in the coach.

Exit MARY.

It's a Volvo. You could sit up front.

Exit JOHN after MARY.

Mary.

Scene 2

Enter JO followed by RALPH.

RALPH: Jo.

JO: No.

RALPH: Come on, I was joking – I didn't really want you to shag him.

JO: So why did you tell him I would?

RALPH: It was a joke.

JO: You wouldn't care.

RALPH: I would.

> *He puts his arms around her.*

Alright.

JO: No.

RALPH: Take your bra off.

JO: No.

RALPH: Let's get married and go to Paris for the weekend.

JO: Alright.

RALPH: Yeah.

> *He kisses her. Enter PAUL. He watches them kissing. JO sees PAUL watching and pushes RALPH off.*

PAUL: He'll be down in a minute, he's putting his trousers on.

JO: I'm sorry if we woke you.

PAUL: You didn't wake me, I wasn't asleep, I don't sleep.

> *Exit PAUL.*

RALPH: You fancy him, don't you?

JO: Don't be soft, he's old enough to be my grandad.

RALPH: Maybe that's who you'd like him to be.

JO: I don't fancy my grandad.

RALPH: Have a gobstopper.

JO: I don't.

RALPH: Have a gobstopper.

JO: You won't get round me like that. Would you really marry me?

RALPH: Maybe, depends.

JO: On what?

RALPH: Take your bra off.

JO: No.

RALPH: Come on.

JO: Not in someone else's front room.

RALPH pulls at her top.

No – don't...

He chases after her.

RALPH: Come on, no one'll know.

JO: Stop it will you, he might come in again.

RALPH: I'll put it down my trousers.

She laughs.

Ah ha, got you, you laughed.

JO: No I never.

RALPH: You laughed I saw you.

JO: I never.

RALPH: You did – you just...

JO: Oh Ralph.

RALPH: What?

JO: What's taking him so long, he's only got to put his trousers on.

RALPH: Go on, take your bra off.

JO: Do you love me?

RALPH: Yeah, of course.

JO: Say it. Go on, say it.

RALPH: I love you.

JO: You don't mean it.

RALPH: Of course I mean it, I wouldn't say it if I didn't mean it, why else would I say it.

JO: Say it again.

RALPH: Ah, Jo.

JO: Just say it Ralph.

RALPH: I love you. What – what are you laughing at?

RALPH gooses JO.

JO: Ralph.

RALPH: You like it.

JO: No.

RALPH: You do.

JO: Someone might come.

RALPH: So what?

RALPH takes off his jacket and shirt.

Whey – hey!

She laughs.

"It's my life!"

RALPH dives onto JO and they fall back onto the sofa. RALPH ravages and tickles her.

JO: No... don't...

RALPH: You love it.

JO: Stop it – Ralph, Ralph, Ralph – I've wet myself.

> *She pushes RALPH off.*

Put your shirt on, someone might come.

RALPH: It's cold.

JO: Put your shirt on then.

RALPH: I don't want to put my shirt on.

JO: Do you love me?

RALPH: No.

> *She kisses him. Enter REG half dressed.*

Ah-ha – Reg matey – how are you doing – good to see you mate.

REG: Now then Jo.

JO: Hello.

RALPH: Have a go if you like – ah-ha!

REG: What day is it?

RALPH: Wednesday.

REG: Yeah, feels like a Wednesday.

JO: I said we should've come later.

RALPH: Have a gobstopper.

REG: No thanks.

RALPH: Go on then Reg – how's things?

REG: Alright – yeah, fine.

RALPH: Great.

REG: How about you?

RALPH: Terrible. No – no it's alright – fucking awful.

REG: Yeah.

JO: You've ripped my bra.

RALPH: Ah, what – I'm mad me, mad, mad, mad.

REG: How are you Jo?

JO: Yeah, great.

RALPH: Go on then – how's things.

REG: Yeah – not good... not good... no good at all.

RALPH: He's still alive then.

REG: Yeah.

They laugh.

RALPH: Don't worry mate, he'll die.

REG: I could kill him.

RALPH: He'll die.

REG: No he won't.

RALPH: He will.

REG: Oh yeah?

RALPH: Yeah, and when he's dead and buried all this will be yours.

JO: Don't talk about his dad like that.

REG: It's council.

RALPH: I love you mate. I love this boy he's magic. The first time I met Reg he was out of his brain and on all fours trying to get out of a pub.

REG: My mother had just died.

RALPH: Yeah, yeah. He was trying to crawl into a cupboard and he grabs my leg and says, "Who am I", I ask you, "Who the fuck am I", what a sad line to come out with to a complete stranger and on all fours.

REG: We went for a curry.

RALPH: Yeah.

JO: When was this?

REG: Just over a year ago.

RALPH: Here, cheer yourself up and have a go if you like.

Exit JO.

No – Jo, wait – wait will you. Look Reg, I've got some more stuff needs delivering, a really big consignment coming in, I'll be right in the shit if you don't do it for us – loads of money, you could get your brother to ride shot gun again, what do you say eh? Living on the edge, life in the fast lane making drops for Ralphey babe. We'll get wrecked.

REG: Yeah, alright.

RALPH: Great, I knew you wouldn't let us down.

RALPH goes to exit.

REG: Ralph.

RALPH: Oh, yeah – my head it's gone, I'm falling apart, bad eyes, bad head, bad all over.

Gives envelope to REG.

It's all there.

REG: I don't have to check it then.

RALPH: He's a good little worker that kid brother of yours.

REG: He's not my brother.

RALPH: Yeah. Give us a ring eh and we'll go for a drink, I'll let you know when the stuff comes in. Every day, I thank God I'm not a woman Reg.

Exit RALPH. REG opens the envelope and counts the money inside.

Scene 3

JOHN listening to 'Are You Lonesome Tonight' by Elvis Presley. Totally absorbed in the mood of the song. At times mouthing the words. He turns up the volume for the last verse and sings along. Enter MARY with a pile of dirty laundry followed by PAUL.

PAUL: I never, I never right – turn that noise off will you –

JOHN turns off the music.

I never hit a woman in my life, not out of spite.

MARY: Only when they deserved it.

JOHN: You don't have to do my washing Mary.

MARY: I'm not. No wonder you never got married, there was no woman desperate or luckless enough to need you.

JOHN: Have a fruit gum Mary.

MARY: You're still here then?

JOHN: Oh, just a couple more days that's all.

MARY: That's what you said last week.

JOHN: You don't want a fruit gum then?

MARY: This place is a pigsty.

Exit MARY

JOHN: My teeth are coming loose.

PAUL: Three times a week that woman comes in to help and three times a week she makes my life hell.

JOHN: I've always had good teeth.

PAUL: Do my arm will you.

JOHN: I haven't got false teeth.

PAUL: All my life I've loved women.

JOHN: The only ones that aren't mine, are these two at the front. Cheer up eh. What?

PAUL: No wonder you've got false teeth.

JOHN: I haven't got false teeth. Have a fruit gum.

PAUL: You've got lousy teeth. (*Takes a fruit gum.*) I'm fat. I drink too much. I'm old. It's summer and I haven't been out in the country, I haven't seen the flowers. I haven't been out for years.

JOHN: She's alright is Mary. She looks after you, she doesn't have to, you only pay her to clean.

PAUL: I don't pay her, the Social pays for her. Get me a drink.

JOHN gives PAUL a large brown envelope.

JOHN: They're not brilliant but I thought you might appreciate them.

PAUL: I need a drink.

JOHN: Mary's got arthritis on her knee, she let me feel it.

PAUL: Old, fat, and ugly.

JOHN: Yeah, well –

PAUL: Get me a drink will you.

JOHN: You're not allowed.

PAUL: You enjoy it, don't you?

JOHN: I'm looking out for you.

PAUL: You always were a nag – all the time we worked together, nag, nag, nag.

JOHN: It's not been the same since you left.

PAUL: I didn't leave, I was sacked.

JOHN: Yeah, sacked. The drivers keep getting younger.

PAUL: It's all over.

JOHN: Yeah.

PAUL: The days of wine and roses are over.

JOHN: Spain.

PAUL: Spain.

JOHN: You like Spain.

PAUL: I loved Spain. What was the name of that bar?

JOHN: What bar?

PAUL: You know… whats-its… you know – T bone steaks as big as your plate piles of chips, as much wine as you can drink, they've got that floor show, exotic dancers, you can get everything you want for a tenner, all in, the owner does magic tricks. I used to sit in that bar all evening and watch the sun go down – his wife organises the Bingo.

JOHN: Margarita's.

PAUL: Margarita's.

JOHN: The last job I had was to Spain. A package holiday, Gravesend to the Costa del Sol.

PAUL coughs.

You want to stop smoking.

PAUL: They'll have to cut off my legs first.

JOHN: Here, you'll like this.

PAUL: Bloody nag.

PAUL takes porn magazines out of envelope and flicks through them.

JOHN: Listen. We were in the coach park loading up, waiting to get off, and this widow turns up all in black, young girl, stunning, her husband had just died. And I says to the lad I'm working with, young lad first time out, I says to him, "she's yours". He doesn't know what I'm on about, hasn't got a clue – like me when I started with you. Are you listening or what?

PAUL: Right, yeah.

JOHN: Anyroad, we set off going along, first stop, and bang she won't get off the coach. So I says to this lad – Phillip, that was his name – I says –

PAUL: Look at the size of that.

JOHN looks at picture.

JOHN: Yeah, yeah – I says "Go on go and get her, I'll give this lot an extra ten minutes to give you time". He still doesn't know what I'm on about, so I get on the coach and there she is on the back seat all in black, sobbing away, tight little skirt, red stilettoes.

PAUL: Oh, I don't like the look of that.

JOHN: I could've had her myself but I says, "Don't worry madam, my colleague will be along any minute now with a nice hot cup of tea."

PAUL: You might as well stick a hat pin through it.

JOHN: It's not a hat pin.

PAUL: Well I couldn't do it.

JOHN: You don't have to.

PAUL: Good.

JOHN: Bloody listen will you. So I get off the coach and I says to this lad, "She's yours she's waiting", and he says, "Waiting for what" and I says, "A cup of tea" – A cup of tea – he didn't have a clue – oh, forget it.

PAUL: Oh aye, yeah, yeah.

JOHN: You don't listen, you never listen.

PAUL: (*Reading.*) "Worldwide hardcore filth, live sex and recorded sex – No more rubbish... Ordinary British Telecom rates – Danish lesbians doing it live."

JOHN: Where?

PAUL: We should give them a ring.

JOHN: Yeah.

PAUL: 01-0852-172-33756, where's that then?

JOHN: Holland.

PAUL: Amsterdam.

JOHN: Denmark.

> *Enter MARY. PAUL stuffs magazines up his shirt.*

Oh, hello Mary.

MARY: Have you taken your tablets?

JOHN: How's your knee?

MARY: You're sure you've taken your tablets. No you haven't.

PAUL: I have.

MARY: No you haven't, they were on the side. You forgot.

PAUL: No I didn't.

JOHN: Where would he be without you Mary.

> *She gives PAUL his tablets.*

MARY: Go on then.

PAUL: I knew something bad was going to happen today, I was waiting for something bad to happen and now it's happened.

JOHN: What's happened?

MARY: You're out of bleach.

PAUL: I need water.

MARY looks at JOHN.

JOHN: Right.

Exit JOHN. MARY plumps up a sofa cushion.

MARY: Move yourself.

PAUL: He fancies you.

MARY: Shift.

PAUL: He's got his eye on you.

MARY: Just shift.

PAUL: He has, he's got his eye on you.

MARY: Just move.

PAUL: Alright.

He gets up. Enter JOHN with water.

JOHN: Here you go Mary.

JOHN gives water to PAUL.

PAUL: You're a hard woman – she's a hard woman.

MARY: Take your tablet.

JOHN: You're a lucky man.

PAUL takes tablets and drinks water. He offers the empty glass to MARY.

PAUL: Thank you.

She doesn't take it.

JOHN: Here let me.

JOHN takes the glass. PAUL lies down on the floor. MARY plumps up the sofa cushions.

If only we were twenty years younger... the young... they've got so much going for them... they're young. No one will have to grow old in the future – fifty years, a hundred years from now... we're on the verge of a revolution – a technological and genetic revolution – you've only got to think how much has changed in our own life times – a hundred years from now and we won't recognise ourselves – we'll be to the future like the ape is to us now – man will evolve into a new species.

MARY: You can sit down again now.

PAUL: I like lying.

JOHN: It's too late for us we're apes.

MARY: You're out of bleach.

PAUL: When are they going to blow up the channel tunnel, that's what I'm wondering.

MARY: I can't finish the kitchen without bleach.

PAUL: Put your feet up woman.

JOHN: Yeah – stay and have a drink with us.

PAUL: Go on.

MARY: I'm not finished in the kitchen.

JOHN: I'll give you a hand if you like.

Exit MARY.

What I'd give to be twenty six again.

Enter MARY with a book.

MARY: You're out of bleach.

She sits and reads. Silence.

JOHN: Do you like Elvis? I like Elvis. We could... only if you like.

Silence.

I'll go and get some bleach. Do you want anything?

PAUL: A Kit Kat.

MARY: He's not allowed.

PAUL: A Kit Kat that's all.

MARY: You eat chocolate and you're dead.

PAUL: For crying out loud woman.

JOHN: Just the bleach then.

PAUL: I'll have a packet of mints. It's only a packet of mints.

JOHN: A packet of mints then.

MARY: You do and you'll kill him.

Exit JOHN.

PAUL: He fancies you.

MARY: The young who's interested in the young.

She reads. Silence.

PAUL: I'm hungry. Come and do my arm for me will you... come on. It's raining. Oh, I feel sick. Come and do my arm will you. Good is it? I'm hungry. What is it? It's raining. What are you reading?

MARY: Feel the Fear and Do It.

PAUL: I haven't got anything to read.

MARY: If you're going to kill yourself, spring's the time to do it, that's when most people do it – not Christmas – just as things look brighter.

PAUL: My arches have fallen. My arches have fallen.

MARY: People kill themselves for three reasons – when they don't feel needed, don't feel loved and there's no hope.

PAUL: I'm hungry.

MARY: Have a biscuit.

PAUL: I don't want a biscuit. Do my arm. I'm hungry.

MARY: Stop going on will you.

PAUL: I'm not.

MARY: You are.

PAUL: I'm not.

MARY: You are.

PAUL: I'm not.

MARY: You are.

PAUL: When I die I don't want burying I want burning. What did you do with your husband?

MARY: I buried him.

PAUL: Poor bloke.

MARY: He was dead.

PAUL: Aye, I bet he was. Where did you bury him?

MARY: Acton.

PAUL: Acton – at least you know where he is, that's more than most wives know about their husbands. Do my arm for me will you – go on. I bet you had smashing legs when you were younger.

She gets up.

Don't go.

Exit MARY. He takes out magazines and looks at one.

You've got lovely legs beautiful legs – make us a sandwich will you.

Enter MARY. PAUL covers up magazines.

MARY: There's no milk.

PAUL: Make me a corned beef sandwich.

MARY: You didn't get any milk.

PAUL: Aye well, I couldn't I had to stay in.

MARY: No wonder you look guilty.

PAUL: I don't feel guilty.

MARY: You look guilty.

PAUL: There's milk I'm telling you – look in the fridge – just look in the fridge will you.

MARY: I gave it to the cat.

PAUL: What for? Let the bugger die.

MARY: You've got no soul.

PAUL: I want a cup of tea.

MARY: You don't know what you want, you want whatever's going. What you need is a good book.

Exit MARY. PAUL hides the magazines under the sofa.

PAUL: I hate that cat. One of these days I'll take it down the canal in a plastic bag and teach it to swim. See if I don't, by the bridge.

Enter MARY with a chocolate biscuit.

Where's mine?

MARY: You said you didn't want one.

PAUL: You think more of that cat than you do of me – your husband should think himself lucky he's dead.

MARY: I'll go and clean for someone else if you like.

PAUL: Coming round here giving next door's cat my milk – I've got no soul – at least I don't go round making a fool of myself hugging trees. Go on then, go – see if I care – go and hug a bloody tree. What do you hug trees for? Well? Why do you hug trees?

MARY: I feel like it.

PAUL: You're fifty years old.

MARY: I know.

PAUL: You want to stop reading those books you do – no good's going to come of all this 'working on yourself', it won't I'm telling you, you hear?

MARY: You, what do you know?

PAUL: I'm only saying it for your own good.

MARY: You don't even know those two boys are yours, not for sure – you can't even go to the shop without breaking into a cold sweat expecting the worst to happen, you can't even get out the front door.

PAUL: I'm not well. (*He lights a cigarette.*)

MARY: 'You're telling me'.

PAUL: I can't breathe.

MARY: Don't smoke then.

PAUL: It's my nerves.

MARY: Go for a walk then.

PAUL: I don't like it out.

MARY: You don't like it anywhere.

He begins to cough and is unable to stop. Enter COLIN and REG.

COLIN: Just give us my money.

REG: What money.

COLIN: Half that money's mine.

MARY slaps PAUL's back trying to get him to stop.

MARY: Get some water.

COLIN: I haven't got any money.

REG: Go back to mini cabbing then.

MARY: Hold your breath and count back from a hundred.

REG: You couldn't even do that.

COLIN: I kept getting lost.

REG: Yeah, London's a big place.

MARY: Get some water.

COLIN: What's the matter with him?

MARY: He's choking.

Exit COLIN.

REG: Shall I ring for an ambulance then?

Enter COLIN. Gives water to MARY. PAUL sips at it slowly and recovers his breath.

So he's not going to die then? He'll be alright?

MARY: Breathe slowly – you'll be alright... it's alright.

COLIN: So where's my money?

REG: What money?

COLIN: The money that Ralph gave you.

REG: He never gave us any money – honest.

MARY: Help me will you.

REG: You help him.

PAUL: I'm alright, I can manage.

COLIN helps MARY with PAUL onto a chair. Exit MARY.

I know what you want. I'll see to you alright.

REG: We're here to look after you dad, you asked us to come and look after you.

COLIN: Yeah.

PAUL: I've got your card marked.

COLIN: Get some rest dad. I haven't got any money.

REG: Get a job then.

COLIN: I went down the Jobcentre but they wouldn't let me in – they said they were closed because of a dangerous carpet.

REG: What's a dangerous carpet look like?

COLIN: I don't know, he wouldn't let us in.

REG: You never went.

COLIN: I went.

REG: Since when has a carpet been dangerous?

COLIN: He said it was dangerous.

REG: Yeah.

COLIN: It's true – honest.

REG: Here you go – fifty – out of my own pocket. Go on take it. (*Door bell rings.*) Take it.

COLIN takes the money.

COLIN: Ta.

Doorbell rings again. Neither of them move. Doorbell rings again.

COLIN: Alright, I'll get it.

Exit COLIN. REG takes out envelope and transfers a wad of cash from it to his wallet.

Soft bugger.

PAUL lies down on the sofa and pulls the sleeping bag over him.

Yeah, it's cold.

Enter COLIN with JULIA. JULIA carries a large suitcase.

COLIN: Sit down if you like.

JULIA: I don't want to be any trouble.

COLIN: This is Julia.

JULIA: Hello.

COLIN: She's come to see Mary.

REG: Reg.

JULIA: Julia.

COLIN: Colin. Sit down if you like.

JULIA: I don't want to be any trouble. (*She sits.*)

REG: That's a big suitcase.

COLIN: It's raining.

REG: Have you come far.

JULIA: No.

COLIN: Summer.

JULIA: Tottenham.

COLIN: That's Paul – he's asleep.

REG: Where are you going?

JULIA: I don't know.

COLIN: Are you going on holiday.

JULIA: No.

COLIN: I don't go on holiday?

REG: You don't go anywhere.

COLIN: I went to Stoke just before Christmas. An uncle of mine got his head chopped off by a propeller. Would you like a cup of tea?

JULIA: I don't want to be any trouble.

REG: I know Tottenham. I had a mate lived in Stamford Hill – he didn't like it. A lot of jews and that. Are you married?

JULIA: Yes.

REG: I'm not. Where's your husband?

COLIN: I'll go and look out the back.

REG: She's not out the back. Do you like football?

JULIA: No.

COLIN: (*Shouts upstairs.*) Mary!

REG: I like football.

COLIN: (*Shouts upstairs.*) Mary!

Enter JOHN.

(*Shouts upstairs.*) There's someone down here come for you.

JOHN: Oh, hello.

REG: A friend of Mary's.

JOHN: Right.

JOHN throws a packet of mints to PAUL.

PAUL: What's this?

JOHN: Trebor mints.

PAUL: I wanted a Kit Kat.

JOHN: You've got mints.

PAUL: I don't like Trebor mints.

JOHN: I'll have them then.

PAUL throws mints at JOHN.

PAUL: I wanted a Kit Kat.

COLIN: (*To JULIA.*) He's not well.

PAUL: I'm fitter than you or him'll ever be.

REG: You're fat.

PAUL: I know you, where do I know you from?

JOHN: She's a friend of Mary's.

PAUL: Give me those mints.

JOHN: You said you didn't want them.

PAUL takes the mints from JOHN.

PAUL: Aren't you ever going to grow up?

JOHN: Not while I'm with you, no.

PAUL: Here have a mint. Go on.

JULIA takes one.

JULIA: Thanks.

PAUL: I wanted a Kit Kat.

Enter MARY.

JULIA: Oh Mum... Mum... Mum.

JULIA bursts into tears.

I'm sorry mum... I'm sorry – You weren't in... I sat in a café... I kept ringing but there wasn't any answer ...

MARY: It's alright, you're alright.

JOHN: I'll go and get a Kit Kat.

COLIN: Yeah.

Exit COLIN and JOHN.

MARY: What are you looking at?

REG: Nothing.

Exit REG. PAUL gives JULIA a dirty tea towel.

PAUL: Here.

JULIA: Thank you.

MARY: It's alright, you're alright.

JULIA: I'm tired.

PAUL: She can have a lie down if you like.

MARY: Come on.

JULIA: I'm alright. There's nothing wrong. I'm tired... You hadn't phoned, I was worried, I wanted to see you were alright.

MARY: I'll make you a sandwich.

JULIA: I'm not hungry.

Exit MARY and JULIA.

Scene 4

JOHN on the phone.

JOHN: Hello sugar, it's me... do you miss me?... I miss you sugar... do you?... do you?... ahh – we're just leaving Aberdeen.

Enter REG with newspaper.

I do, I do... of course I do sugar, bye, bye, bye. (*Puts phone down.*)

The wife.

REG: There's a bloke walking round the Midlands somewhere, with an ear sewn to the inside of his thigh – he forgot to turn up to have it stitched back onto his head.

JOHN: Oh.

REG: Not the sort of thing you forget, is it?

JOHN: No. Mary's daughter eh. Bit of a turn up for the books that.

REG: What?

JOHN: Oh, don't get me wrong.

REG: What?

JOHN: Goodness, is that the time?

REG: Are you expecting a call?

JOHN: Seven o'clock already.

Exit REG. JOHN dials.

Hello sugar, it's me – I'm just ringing from the hotel... I miss you too sugar, we're just leaving Aberdeen... I love you too sugar.

Enter REG with a bag of carrots.

I do, I do sugar – bye, bye, bye.

REG: I love carrots.

REG reads his newspaper and eats a carrot. Banging from upstairs.

Do you want one?

JOHN: No thanks.

Banging from upstairs.

PAUL: (*Offstage.*) Reg... Reg... where are you Reg? I need you Reg – I'm dying!

REG: I'll kill the bugger if he isn't.

Exit REG. JOHN dials.

JOHN: Hello sugar it's me, I'm just ringing from the hotel to say... in Scotland... why would I say I was in Scotland if I wasn't?... we're just leaving Aberdeen ...

PAUL: (*Offstage.*) No, Reg, no, please Reg.

Crash of china and cutlery.

JOHN: An angry waiter... no, you can't ring me... you know why... the phone on the coach isn't for domestic use... I'll lose my job... Look, I miss you sugar... don't say that... it's my job... I don't like being away from home... I love you sugar.

Enter REG.

No, don't ring the yard... I do, I do.

JOHN puts the phone down.

The wife. Is everything alright?

REG: Yeah.

Exit REG. Enter JULIA and MARY.

MARY: You've lost weight. You look tired.

JULIA: I've just woke up.

MARY: You're not looking after yourself –

JULIA: I'm alright.

JOHN goes to exit.

JOHN: I have to go. It's gone seven and I haven't eaten – I
don't suppose... No – I'll get a bag of chips instead. Nice to
have met you ...

JULIA: Julia.

JOHN: Yes, Julia.

Exit JOHN. Silence.

JULIA: You stopped ringing. Why didn't you ring?

MARY: I've had trouble with my legs.

JULIA: I was worried.

MARY: Don't sniff.

JULIA: I'm not sniffing.

MARY: Here – blow your nose. (*Gives JULIA a handkerchief.*)

JULIA: I don't want to blow my nose.

MARY: Blow your nose.

JULIA: Oh, Mum. (*JULIA blows her nose.*) I was worried.

MARY: I'm alright. Something's wrong, there's something
wrong, what's wrong?

JULIA: Nothing.

MARY: You've walked out.

JULIA: No.

MARY: How is your husband?

JULIA: Alright. (*JULIA wipes her nose with her sleeve.*)

MARY: Use your handkerchief.

JULIA: Look, I'll go if you want.

MARY: I'll make you some soup.

JULIA: I'm not hungry.

MARY: What's the matter?

JULIA: Nothing.

MARY: If you had any sense you would, you'd leave him. Alright. What goes on between you and your husband is your business, don't tell me, I don't want to know.

JULIA: Everything's fine.

MARY: I can't help it, I worry. You can tell me, whatever it is, I don't mind, I'm your mother.

JULIA: There's nothing to worry about – I just need to get away that's all... I wanted to see you were alright, I was worried – you stopped coming round, you didn't ring.

MARY: I've had trouble with my legs.

Enter PAUL.

PAUL: Oh, don't mind me – you carry on.

MARY: We were just going.

JULIA: I'm sorry about earlier... I was tired.

PAUL: Oh, that's alright. I never forget a pretty face.

PAUL takes envelope with magazines out from under the sofa.

Tax returns.

MARY: Julia's coming to stay with me for a while.

PAUL: Oh, that'll be nice.

JULIA: Yeah.

PAUL unplugs the phone.

PAUL: I've got some calls to make.

MARY: It's alright, we're going.

PAUL: Oh no, I'll make them from my bed – in the bedroom. Colin put a new socket in for me – he's very good with his hands that boy – must take after his mother. Oh well, I expect I'll be seeing you around then.

JULIA: Yeah.

Exit PAUL.

Scene 5

Early afternoon. A few cans of beer on the table. COLIN, RALPH, REG and JO. COLIN in a shirt and boxer shorts. JO sketching. RALPH practising with golf club and ball, with a mug turned on its side for the hole.

COLIN: If I had a sister she wouldn't be your sister. She'd be my sister. Have you got a sister?

REG: No.

RALPH: You should take up painting again.

JO: I don't paint anymore.

COLIN: If you had a sister –

REG: I haven't got a sister.

RALPH: No, I'm serious, you liked doing that.

JO: I don't paint.

RALPH: You were good at it.

COLIN: I could marry your sister.

REG: No you bloody couldn't.

COLIN: Why not.

REG: Because you couldn't.

COLIN: Who says?

REG: I says.

JO: I don't paint anymore, only in my head, I paint with my head.

RALPH: Alright.

COLIN: Why couldn't I marry your sister?

REG: I haven't got a sister.

COLIN: Yeah but ...

RALPH: What's the matter with you?

JO: I hate golf.

Exit JO.

RALPH: Everyday I thank God I'm not a woman.

COLIN: You could be best man.

REG: I wouldn't come, I'd kill you first.

COLIN: What about your sister, you wouldn't want to upset your sister.

REG: You leave my sister alone.

COLIN: We'd go on honeymoon, somewhere sexy, I'd tell you all about it – me and your sister.

REG: I haven't got a sister, right.

COLIN: Right.

REG: So leave her alone.

COLIN: I wouldn't want to marry your sister anyway. She'd be ugly like you.

RALPH gets ball in hole.

RALPH: Yes, yes, yes – "It's my life!"

COLIN: Aye, aye, he's off again.

RALPH: Whey-hey – Reggie, Reggie, Reggie – Colin, my old mate – mates – I love you. How are you doing mate?

REG: Alright mate, alright.

COLIN: You're not his mate.

RALPH: Ha – ha – ha, matey.

COLIN: Don't call me matey, I'm not your mate.

RALPH: This is my lucky day boys.

RALPH looks at watch.

So where's the old man then?

REG: Sleeping.

COLIN: Yeah, that's what he does.

RALPH checks his watch again and shows it to REG.

RALPH: Is that the time?

REG looks at RALPH's watch and then his own.

REG: No.

RALPH: What time is it?

COLIN: Time you got another watch.

REG: Colin.

COLIN: What?

RALPH: My watch has stopped, what time is it?

REG: Quarter past three.

RALPH: It's late, I'm going to be late... Oh no, this is terrible – where's the nearest bookies?

COLIN: On the High Street.

REG: You've got a bet on. Why didn't you say?

RALPH: I just did.

REG: You could've said.

RALPH: I've said – the three fory at Kempton, I haven't put it on yet, I'm going to be late.

COLIN: So go and put it on then. It's only round the corner. I don't see what the problem is. What's the problem?

REG: There is no problem.

RALPH: Go and wake him up.

REG: No.

COLIN: What's going on?

REG: Nothing's going on.

COLIN: Where's Jo gone? She's alright is Jo, I like Jo.

RALPH: Have her if you like – go on, have her, have a cigar, enjoy yourself, have a sherbert dip.

RALPH offers COLIN a sherbert dip. COLIN takes the sherbert dip.

COLIN: Ta.

RALPH: Do you ever wake up and not know who you are? I get that. The sheer terror and panic of not knowing – you can't imagine, not even in your worst dreams – and then I remember and I feel dreadful, bad, really awful... One day

I'll wake up and I won't remember. It's worrying.

COLIN: Yeah, you haven't paid up yet.

REG looks at RALPH.

REG: No, you haven't.

COLIN: How is Vincent?

RALPH: Vincent.

COLIN: Fat Vincent.

RALPH: Oh, yeah, Fat Vincent. (*To REG.*) Here, would you like to piss on someone?

REG: (*Looks at COLIN.*) Yeah.

RALPH: (*To COLIN.*) Who would you like to piss on?

COLIN: (*Looks at REG.*) Cheers.

COLIN drinks a beer.

RALPH: I'd like to piss on that American actress... you know... in the bathing costume on telly... she reminds me of a fish-finger. Whey-hey! (*Pours can of beer on his head and sings.*) "It's my life – It's my life –" (*Falls to the floor.*) Walk on me... walk on my chest.

Enter JO.

JO: What's going on?

COLIN: He wants us to walk on his chest.

JO: Oh not again – I hate it when you get like this.

RALPH: I'm happy. I feel dreadful, awful – oh, oh, no – I just realised boys, I don't have a positive outlook on life. It's terrible. I've felt like this ever since I left home – there's only one woman ever loved me properly and that's my mother.

COLIN looks at JO's sketch.

COLIN: That's good that is.

JO: Thanks.

COLIN: You should take it up professionally.

JO: I'm only good at cartoons.

RALPH: We're stuck mate, stuck in a lift that's stuck and no one's coming to get us and the floors dropped out. Everything's stuck.

REG: Yeah.

RALPH: You'll be alright.

COLIN: I like watching.

RALPH: Don't worry mate, don't worry. Uncle Ralph'll see you alright – have a sherbet dip.

REG takes one.

COLIN: You're clever you.

JO: Oh yeah.

COLIN: Yeah.

JO: No I'm not.

COLIN: Yes you are.

JO: I haven't got any brains I'm stupid.

COLIN: You go to college – you can't be that stupid – you've got to have brains to go to college. You should make his belly bigger than that.

REG: My idea of hell, right – this big black emptiness that goes on forever, infinite, nothing, and you're floating in the middle of it and you're stuck in your own head in this big black emptiness.

COLIN: Then what, after college like?

JO: I don't know, I'd like to work with the disabled.

COLIN: I like your shirt.

JO: Have you got any left?

COLIN: What – oh, yeah. (*Gives her his beer.*) It goes with your eyes.

JO: Does it?

COLIN: Yeah.

REG: Go and put your trousers on Colin.

COLIN: How was Redhill Ralph?

RALPH: You what?

JO: Give him his money Ralph.

RALPH: What money?

COLIN: (*To JO.*) His belly still isn't big enough.

Enter PAUL.

PAUL: What's going on?

REG: Nothing. Where have you been?

PAUL: Nowhere.

REG: This is Ralph Dad.

RALPH: Nice to meet you.

PAUL: All my life I've lived where it's Labour and now... New Labour – New Labour!... Where do you live?

RALPH: Westminster.

PAUL: Yeah. Go to hell. To hell with the lot of them. There's nothing worth fighting for now.

RALPH: You've got a lovely house Paul, you're a very lucky man.

COLIN: Yeah, dead lucky.

REG: Go and make some tea Colin.

COLIN: There's no milk.

PAUL: There's never any milk.

COLIN: Don't look at me, what about him.

PAUL: It's too cold to go out.

RALPH: It's a beautiful house.

COLIN: All it needs is some furniture.

PAUL: Are you complaining?

COLIN: Yeah.

REG: Make the tea Colin.

COLIN: There's no milk.

PAUL: You don't like it, pack your bags.

COLIN: Miserable old –

REG: Colin.

COLIN: What – what – don't look at me, why's it always me, I haven't done anything.

REG: Put your trousers on.

RALPH: Late Victorian.

PAUL: Council.

JO: (*To COLIN.*) You should undo this button, you've got a lovely hairy chest.

RALPH: You should buy it.

PAUL: What for? I haven't got any money.

COLIN: Oh aye. What? You've got beautiful eyes.

JO: Thank you.

REG: Ralph's a business man dad.

RALPH: Something you can pass on.

PAUL: I'm not leaving these buggers anything, I know what you think and that's fine by me but you're not getting a penny.

COLIN: Oh aye – money, you've got money.

REG: Make the tea Colin.

COLIN: You make it.

RALPH: It's got a lot of the original fittings and fixtures.

PAUL: The Council hasn't spent a penny on it.

COLIN: He won't even switch the telly on, just sits and looks at it, thinking how much he's saved by not plugging it in.

JO: Undo your button.

REG: Ralph's a businessman.

PAUL: Good for you.

JO: You have, you've got a lovely hairy chest.

RALPH: Look Paul, you don't mind me calling you Paul do you?

JO: Go on.

COLIN undoes shirt button.

RALPH: You can't lose with property, it's a sound financial investment.

JO: That looks nice.

COLIN: All property is theft.

REG: Go and put your trousers on Colin.

COLIN: I'm serious.

REG: So am I – put your trousers on.

COLIN: What for?

REG: It's embarrassing, you're embarrassing Jo.

COLIN: No I'm not.

RALPH: Yes you are.

JO: No he's not.

RALPH: Shut up Jo.

COLIN: Don't talk to her like that.

RALPH: Like what?

COLIN: Like that.

PAUL: Behave yourself Colin, we've got guests.

COLIN: What's going on, there's something going on.

REG: There's nothing going on.

COLIN: Something's up.

REG: Nothing's up, right.

COLIN: Right.

REG: So go and put your trousers on.

COLIN: You take your trousers off.

REG: What the fuck are you on.

PAUL: Right, that's enough boys, we'll have none of that language in here. Go and put your trousers on Colin.

COLIN: Look at you – you're all so, so, so, – (*To REG.*) I'd hate to be in your head man – a pea rattling about in a small empty metal bowl – you know what your trouble is don't you, you've got no sense of fun – you can't laugh at yourself. Go on, give us a smile, come on. No, you've got nothing to smile about. You've got no heart. Give us your wallet Ralph, come on, give it us and smile.

PAUL: Go and put your trousers on.

COLIN: Alright, I'm going. You have you've got beautiful eyes.

Exit COLIN. A loud sharp burst of a pavement drill is heard from out back. RALPH ducks instinctively. The drill stops.

RALPH: No wonder he hasn't got any trousers on, he probably doesn't know which way up they go without a diagram.

JO: God, you're arrogant, an arrogant bully.

RALPH: Me, what me, what have I done?

Exit JO. A longer prolonged burst of the drill. Exit PAUL.

REG: He's not interested.

RALPH: What?

Drill stops.

REG: He's not interested.

RALPH: I haven't done anything.

REG: He'll never agree to it.

RALPH: He'll agree to anything. Stupid cow.

REG: He won't I'm telling you.

RALPH: Of course he will.

Sharp burst of drill.

PAUL: (*Offstage.*) You're killing me with that thing.

RALPH: Look, what chance has he got of getting a mortgage at his age? Zeroissimo. He needs you.

REG: He's not interested.

RALPH: He's interested. He needs you to get the mortgage.

REG: But I haven't got any money.

RALPH: You don't need money, I've got money. You get the mortgage, I act as guarantor. The Council won't sell it to me. They'll sell it to you for at least fifty percent of the market value, probably less, because you're family and he's lived here so long. Then we sell and realise its full value and split the loot, you and me mate, we'll make a killing.

REG: Yeah.

RALPH: If it was a horse I'd bet on it. What time is it?

REG: Half past three.

Drill starts.

PAUL: (*Offstage.*) You're killing me, I'm a sick old man.

Drill stops.

MAN'S VOICE: (*Offstage.*) Bugger off and drop dead then grandad.

RALPH: Who knows, with a bit of luck he might drop dead.

REG: Yeah.

They laugh. Drilling starts again. Enter PAUL.

Would you like a cup of tea Dad.

RALPH: I'd best be going then. Good to have met you Paul.

RALPH shakes PAUL's hand. Drilling stops.

Where's the nearest bookies?

REG: On the High Street. Put a fiver on for us.

PAUL: You're having a bet.

RALPH: It's a dead cert Paul, can't lose.

PAUL: Here, put a pound on for me.

He searches his pockets for a pound with no luck. REG gives RALPH a pound.

REG: Here.

PAUL: Thanks son.

RALPH: Don't worry I'll see myself out.

Exit RALPH.

REG: I'll put the kettle on then.

PAUL: What for?

REG: Go on, put your feet up.

PAUL: I'm not tired.

REG: Put your feet up.

PAUL lies on sofa.

PAUL: They're digging up the road, they're digging my grave.

REG puts sleeping bag over PAUL.

They're killing me.

REG: Yeah.

REG turns on the radio: Seligkeit by Schubert, sung by Elly Ameling.

PAUL: What's this?

REG: I don't know.

PAUL: Funeral music.

REG: I'll change it if you like.

PAUL: No turn it up.

REG: I'll make the tea.

Exit REG.

PAUL: Oh God, I'm dying.

PAUL draws sleeping bag over his head. Drilling starts.

ACT TWO

Scene 6

Hot summer's day. On the table the aftermath of a picnic style lunch. JO, COLIN, RALPH, REG and JULIA. RALPH is tuning a small transistor.

JULIA: I was eight years old when my father died. May Bank Holiday. He died in a car crash. He was drunk and I was sat in the back. I didn't speak for months after, I pretended to be a dog.

JO: Do you think there's going to be a heatwave?

REG: I've never liked Bank Holidays.

COLIN: If you stood under an electricity pylon long enough you'd get leukaemia.

REG: What for?

COLIN: I don't know – nuclear power.

REG: Why don't you go and try it.

JO: I'd rather be too hot than too cold.

RALPH: Bloody thing.

REG: Have a smartie.

COLIN: No thanks, they're made by Nestles.

REG: Since when haven't you liked Smarties?

JO: What sort of dog?

REG: What's wrong with Nestles?

JO: They force women in the third world to feed their babies with powdered milk.

RALPH: Bollocks.

REG: Who says?

JO: It's true.

   REG throws a smartie at COLIN's nose.

COLIN: Get off.

REG: You've got the nose.

JO: What nose?

REG: The nose, his dad's nose.

COLIN: It's not his nose, this is my nose, right. He's not my dad.

REG: Who is your dad?

COLIN: I don't know.

JO: I don't shop at Boots, they use animals to test their cosmetics on.

REG: Doesn't your mam know who your dad is?

COLIN: What are you saying about my mam?

REG: Nothing.

RALPH: Bloody work will you.

COLIN: Don't talk about my mam like that.

REG: Like what?

JO: I think your dad's quite sexy.

COLIN: He's not my dad.

JO: Alright.

REG: (*To JULIA.*) Are you alright? You look a bit off colour. Come and sit over here if you like.

COLIN: As soon as he's dead, I'll be on the first train home to Coventry.

JO: Is that where your mam lives?

COLIN: Yeah.

REG: (*To JULIA.*) Have a smartie.

JO: I've never been to Coventry.

REG: Go on.

JULIA takes a smartie.

JO: I want to see the world.

COLIN: Yeah.

RALPH: I can't get Long Wave.

REG: So, you've left your husband.

JULIA: Have I – who says?

RALPH: I'm missing the first day of the cricket.

REG: So you haven't then?

JULIA: No.

REG: But Mary said.

JULIA: She said wrong.

REG: But she's your mam.

COLIN: Imagine if this was your whole life.

RALPH tunes into a pop station.

JO: How do you mean.

COLIN: If your whole life flashed in front of you right now.

RALPH: Is that the Four Tops?

JO: And then what?

RALPH: Is it?

COLIN: Nothing.

RALPH: It is.

REG: My mam's dead.

JULIA: Oh, I'm sorry.

REG: She died of cancer.

RALPH: It is, it's the Four Tops.

RALPH smashes the radio. The music stops.

REG: It's a dead cert, it can't lose, that's the last time I let you give me a tip.

Exit COLIN.

Have you got any kids?

JULIA: A little boy and a little girl.

REG: One of each.

JULIA: Yeah.

JO: I like your boots.

JULIA: Thanks.

REG: I've got a kid. What's the matter?

JULIA: Nothing.

REG: He's great – I never see him mind – it's his mother, we don't get on, she moved to Newcastle.

RALPH: It's the cricket, I'm missing the cricket.

JO: So, not the end of the world is it?

RALPH: You don't understand.

JO: I hate cricket.

REG: You don't say much do you.

RALPH: Look at you, all you can do is sit around snivelling about animal rights, feeling sorry for yourself.

JO: Oh go and throw your boomerang on the common.

RALPH: Right, right, right – I will.

Exit RALPH.

JO: What sort of music do you like?

JULIA: I don't know – anything.

JO: I bet you like soul.

JULIA: What makes you say that?

JO: I'm intuitive. Do you?

JULIA: Yes.

REG: I like soul music. So, what are your kids called?

Exit JULIA.

JO: Do you?

REG: What? Oh, yeah, yeah.

JO: I've got the Motown Story at home, I'll lend it you if you like.

REG: Yeah, thanks.

Enter MARY and JOHN.

JOHN: We weren't lost I'm telling you.

MARY: What do you call it then?

JOHN: I knew where we were.

MARY: Where's everyone gone?

JOHN sits on sofa.

JOHN: Come and sit down.

MARY: I'm alright.

JOHN: Come on.

MARY: I like standing.

Enter PAUL.

JOHN: It's bad for your legs.

MARY: There's nothing wrong with my legs.

PAUL: I can't go on, I can't.

PAUL sits on the sofa next to JOHN. Exit JO.

JOHN: Where's she going, why can't we all stick together?

PAUL: I wanted to feed the ducks.

JOHN: Move will you.

MARY: (*Looking out the window.*) Look at it.

JOHN: Here, have a fag.

PAUL: I'm never going out again. What's this?

JOHN: That's all they had.

MARY: Just look at it.

JOHN breaks off the tips.

PAUL: Bloody tips.

MARY: People with dogs should be shot.

PAUL: What – I never said anything, don't look at me, what have I done, I haven't done anything I haven't got a dog.

They light up.

MARY: If it was dogs they were murdering and torturing in Bosnia they'd soon put a stop to it people wouldn't stand for it, they'd drop a bomb on the lot of them, a bomb that didn't kill dogs.

JOHN: Why can't we all stick together?

PAUL: When I die I want to die in the open air, looking up at the sky on a day like this.

JOHN: Listening to Elvis.

PAUL: I don't like Elvis.

JOHN: I like Elvis.

PAUL: Find some other bloody place to die then.

REG: You never go out.

PAUL: I don't like going out. It's too big.

REG: You're not dying.

PAUL: I'm dying.

REG: I'll take you out every day if you think it'll help. Have a sweet.

MARY: Have you taken your tablet.

PAUL: Have I?

MARY: No, you haven't.

PAUL: Oh, no – I'll have a sweet instead. I'll take it later.

REG: Just one won't hurt.

He gives PAUL a handful of sweets.

MARY: Well don't come to me when your blood-sugar's gone mad and you can hardly string a sentence together.

JOHN: Fifty years from now they'll have found a cure for death – it won't do us any good, it's too late for us – but our children's children, they won't have to die – it'll change the world. Who knows what they'll know in fifty years. We're like earthworms, we work, we eat, we breed, we die – what's the difference?

MARY: I'm not an earthworm.

REG: She's alright your Julie.

MARY: Julia.

REG: Yeah.

MARY: You keep away.

REG: I'm only saying.

MARY: I know what you're saying.

PAUL: Look at me, I'm falling apart, even my body's a failure.

REG: You owe me a pound.

>   *Exit REG.*

MARY: We all get old.

JOHN: You're not old.

MARY: I am.

JOHN: You're not old – you look great – you do – it's all in the mind – look, you wouldn't say that if you were a millionaire – he wouldn't feel a failure.

MARY: How do you know?

JOHN: Because you wouldn't.

MARY: I'd have a facelift.

JOHN: You don't need a facelift, you look great. You do, you look bloody great for your age.

>   *MARY takes a piece of chocolate cake off the table and eats it.*

>   (*To PAUL.*) Come on.

>   *Enter JULIA.*

JULIA: You'll get fat.

MARY: I like chocolate cake.

JOHN: We're going to feed the ducks.

PAUL: I'm hungry.

JOHN: You're always hungry.

PAUL: I don't want to go out again.

JOHN: We're feeding the ducks.

JOHN pulls PAUL up.

PAUL: You're enjoying this, aren't you?

JOHN: Yes.

PAUL: All the blood's gone to my head.

Exit JOHN and PAUL. Silence.

JULIA: There's a circus on the common.

Silence.

MARY: I miss the sea. All the time I've lived here, I've missed the sea. I couldn't wait to get out. I waited till I was twenty one. And then I came down here. I was lost when I met your father, he went out of his way to see that I got home safely. I miss the sea.

JULIA cries. MARY holds her and comforts her. Enter JO. MARY lets go of JULIA and gives her a hanky.

JO: I was looking for Colin. You haven't seen him then?

MARY: No.

Exit JO.

JULIA: I don't want your hanky.

MARY: Wipe your eyes.

JULIA: You can't just – I don't want it.

JULIA throws away hanky.

You've never been able to have you, not even as a kid – just that look.

MARY: What look?

JULIA: That look. Just that look, or you smothered me.

MARY: What look – what, what do you want me to say?

MARY picks up hanky.

Here, wipe your eyes. Oh, stop sulking.

JULIA: I'm not sulking.

MARY: Why won't you tell me.

JULIA: What, tell you what? Why did you tell them I'd left my husband?

MARY: I don't like him, I never liked him, he's bone idle, I told you not to marry him – he's like your father.

JULIA: Don't.

MARY: All he thought he had to do was smile and everthing was alright.

JULIA: Don't start.

MARY: He made me feel it was all alright.

JULIA: Please don't.

MARY: And then he died.

JULIA: Don't. You had an affair.

MARY: I did nothing wrong. You should divorce your husband now, before it's too late.

JULIA: I don't want my kids growing up the way I did.

MARY: You're father never divorced me – he didn't have it in him.

JULIA: No. You stopped coming round. You don't ring any more. There's never any answer, you're always out.

MARY: I have to work.

JULIA: You could just ring. You stopped coming round.

MARY: Your house is always full, it's too full, full of people – big loud men yabbering on in their own language – I wouldn't even get a cup of tea if I didn't remind you I was there.

JULIA: That's not true.

MARY: I feel like a bit of old furniture shoved up in the corner.

Enter PAUL and JOHN.

JOHN: Are you alright love?

JULIA: Yes, thanks.

JOHN: Here, have a serviette.

Gives her a serviette.

JULIA: Thank you.

Exit JULIA.

MARY: Julia.

She's feeling sick.

PAUL: She feels sick – she should try having my stomach.

PAUL sits and takes a sandwich.

JOHN: We got to the zebra crossing and we had to come
back. We could go out later if you like – make a May Bank
Holiday night of it.

MARY: What about your wife?

PAUL: I can't eat this.

JOHN: It's Karaoke night down the pub. I'll be honest with
you, Mary.

PAUL: It's got pickle on.

JOHN: My wife doesn't understand me Mary – she never has.

PAUL: I can't eat pickle.

JOHN: Don't eat it then.

PAUL eats the sandwich.

I can talk to you Mary, really talk to you. I should
never have married my wife in the first place, it's all
over – even the shouting – all we've got left is the
ring, what's in a ring? The only place that I've got
that I can really call home is my coach. We had to
get married, you know – well, it was a different world
then... we all make mistakes – I mean, I don't have to
tell you that do I.

Exit MARY.

No, I admire you – I do, I really do Mary.

PAUL: Pickled anything gives me chronic wind and
indigestion. It's these bloody tablets, I was alright till I

started on them, I could eat anything and everthing.

JOHN: You're a fat pig, you know that don't you.

PAUL: Watch it, eh.

JOHN: Oh aye?

Takes a sandwich.

I'd like to see you try.

PAUL: That's the last one.

JOHN: So?

PAUL: You wouldn't know what hit you.

JOHN: You are, you're fat.

Enter COLIN, REG, and RALPH.

COLIN: It's not my fault – you said it'd come back.

REG: Yeah – but not if you throw it up a bloody tree it won't.

COLIN: I've never thrown a boomerang before.

RALPH: Boys, boys, it's only a boomerang. Paul me old mate, how are you doing?

PAUL: I'm hungry.

RALPH: We thought you'd got lost.

PAUL: He got lost.

JOHN: I knew where we were.

REG: What's up with Mary?

JOHN: Watch it eh – I was in the merchant navy for five years.

REG: So?

JOHN: I'll knock your block off any more of that.

REG: I never said anything.

JOHN: Right.

JOHN takes off his jacket.

Come on. Try me. Just try me.

Enter JO.

JO: What's going on here then?

REG: Nothing.

JOHN: I'll teach you to take the piss sonny jim.

REG: I'm not.

JOHN: You are.

REG: I'm not.

RALPH: Boys, have champagne instead.

JOHN: I don't want champagne.

REG: What do you want?

JOHN: You –

Enter JULIA supported by MARY.

I'll have you, see if I don't.

JOHN goes to help MARY with JULIA. Exit RALPH.

JO: I've been looking for you.

COLIN: I've lost his boomerang.

JO: Good.

PAUL: (*Suddenly waking from a daydream.*) No – no – not for me thanks, I've had enough.

JULIA: It's alright – I'm alright.

REG: Need any help?

JOHN: No.

Enter RALPH. He pops open a bottle of champagne.

RALPH: Whey-hey – champagne – get some cups Jo.

JO: Drop dead.

RALPH: A real little fire-cracker Paul, she's alright really. Here, you could do with some of that – have some champagne.

RALPH pours himself and PAUL some champagne.

MARY: I can't believe you fell over, a grown woman and you can't even stand up without falling over.

JULIA: I didn't do it on purpose.

MARY: You're always falling over.

JULIA: It was an accident.

RALPH: Champagne.

>*RALPH toasts PAUL.*

REG: Let's have a look.

JOHN: Leave it to me love, I've had experience of these things.

RALPH: What's mine is yours Paul, whatever you want it's yours.

PAUL: What I want is a Socialist to vote for.

JULIA: Aarrgh.

JOHN: Keep still.

REG: He was in the merchant navy.

COLIN: (*To JO.*) Do you believe in God?

>*JO takes out a bottle of olive oil and rubs it into her face and hands.*

PAUL: I put a pound on that horse of yours.

>*RALPH gives PAUL a fiver.*

RALPH: Have it on me mate.

PAUL: Oh, I haven't got any change.

RALPH: I love you Paul, I love you.

MARY: We'll miss the brass band now.

JULIA: I'll go home if you want.

MARY: Don't talk to me like that, I'm your mother.

JULIA: Right.

MARY: Right.

>*RALPH puts arm around PAUL and kisses him on the cheek.*

PAUL: Get off will you, what do you think I am.

RALPH: A mate.

JOHN: It's nothing serious – no bones broke.

MARY: She's just making a fuss, she's always making a fuss.

JULIA: I'll go home on Tuesday.

COLIN: There is no God.

REG: Oy Colin.

COLIN: What?

JO: Do you want some olive oil.

COLIN: No, thanks.

JO: You'd look nice with a tan.

COLIN: You think so?

JO: Yeah.

> *He takes olive oil. She exits and COLIN follows.*

RALPH: You're sitting on a goldmine Paul, it's a buyer's market out there my old son. Here, have another drink – let's drink to your house – and because it's council you get it at below the market price, it's a bargain.

PAUL: I'm old and I haven't got any money.

RALPH: I've got money.

> *JO and COLIN laugh offstage.*

PAUL: What line of business are you in?

REG: I wouldn't stand for it Ralph.

RALPH: I'm a businessman Paul, like Al Capone – no, only joking – I mainly deal in IT – Information Technology.

REG: He sells computer software, I deliver computers for him.

RALPH: It's better than being on the dole.

REG: I am on the dole.

JOHN: It's amazing, you'd never think you were mother and daughter – you look like sisters.

> *JO laughs offstage.*

REG: You've already lost your boomerang.

RALPH: Just go and give everyone a drink will you.

REG: Fine by me pal.

REG picks up champagne and two cups.

JOHN: You do, you look just like your mum.

JULIA: I look like my dad.

JOHN: You've got your mother's eyes.

REG gives a cup to JULIA, keeps the other to himself and pours the champagne. RALPH slaps his hand on PAUL's knee and shakes it firmly and doesn't take it off.

RALPH: Paul.

PAUL: Ralph. Here Reg, have you got change of a fiver.

REG: No. There's only two cups.

JOHN: That's alright, you have it Mary.

MARY: No, you have it.

JOHN: No, no, I don't want it – you have it.

A brass band strikes up in the distance.

MARY: I'm going to listen to the band.

Exit MARY.

JOHN: Hang on, I'll come with you.

Exit JOHN.

REG: Cheers then.

REG and JULIA drink.

RALPH: I love you Paul.

PAUL: It's for that pound I owe you.

REG: Keep it.

PAUL: Thanks.

REG: How is it?

REG gently touches her ankle.

JULIA: Alright, yeah, alright.

REG massages her ankle.

PAUL: I love brass bands.

RALPH: Yes.

RALPH takes his hand off PAUL's knee.

REG: You've got lovely ankles.

JULIA: I'm going home.

REG: Come on, I'll help you outside.

JULIA: I can manage thanks.

REG puts his arm round JULIA's waist and helps her off.

PAUL: So, you'll put up the money for me to by my own house.

RALPH: Let's have another drink.

PAUL: And where does Reg fit in?

RALPH: He doesn't – ah-ha! No, he doesn't. We'll get a better price if we buy direct through you. How long have you lived here?

PAUL: Over twenty years.

RALPH: They'll sell to you for at least a third of the market value. I'll put up the cash and we'll buy it outright.

PAUL: Then what?

RALPH: Oh, we'll sort something out. You'll live rent free for the rest of your life. Have a drink.

PAUL: No thanks.

RALPH: You leave the house to me in your will. Don't worry about the boys, I'll see they're alright.

Enter COLIN and JO.

COLIN: Ou est la boulangerie?

JO: We could go to Paris.

COLIN: Yeah.

PAUL: I'm going to listen to the band.

RALPH: Yeah, great idea, smashing.

PAUL: I love brass bands.

RALPH: Yeah.

Exit PAUL and RALPH. JO undoes COLIN's top button.

COLIN: Right. I forgot.

JO takes off her top. She is wearing a bra.

The band's started.

She rubs olive oil into her chest.

JO: I love the sun.

COLIN: I'll do your back for you, if you like.

She turns. COLIN rubs olive oil into her back.

JO: I love the sun. I'm a sun worshipper.

COLIN: Yeah. You've got a lovely body.

She turns and puts her arms round his neck.

JO: Can you feel it.

COLIN: What?

JO: The sun.

COLIN: Yeah.

JO: Yeah.

She kisses him.

RALPH: (*Offstage.*) Jo!

JO: Come on.

RALPH: (*Offstage.*) Jo!

JO: Let's go for a swim.

COLIN: Yeah.

Exit COLIN and JO.

RALPH: (*Offstage.*) Jo! Jo!

Scene 7

Enter JULIA soaked. Throws off her coat and picks up telephone and dials.

JULIA: No... no... no ...

Slams down phone.

Bloody phone, bloody summer, bloody rain, bloody life!

Collapses in a heap and sobs. Enter JO with umbrella and bunch of keys.

JO: Oh, hello. You're wet. I've got an umbrella.

JULIA: I got caught, I was just ...

JO: Summer. Someone left these in the door. I'll put them on the table.

JO puts keys on the table.

I thought you'd gone home. I'm waiting for Colin. I'll wait here then. You don't mind? Do you want me to get you anything?

JULIA: I'm alright.

JO: Fifty years from now and we'll all be dead, everyone, it'll be the end of the world.

JULIA: Don't ever... don't... don't – they think they can just... and who has to be there... who's left... well I won't – I won't – I won't – I won't... He thinks he can just – I'll always be there – clean house, clean sheets... I'm out the door and... I could rip him apart with my teeth... I'm out the door and he's bringing home the bacon, in like flynn with that piece of trash... I opened the door – there he was, naked, coming out of the bathroom, her shoes on the landing, her clothes on my bed and she's wrapped in a towel hopping about on the landing drying herself down and he said, "Let's talk", "Let's talk" – I'll bloody talk to him alright... Don't ever get married, don't ever have children.

JO: No, I won't. You've left your husband.

JULIA: I'll wring his bloody neck – his devious, two timing, deceitful, scraggy little neck. He needs time, he needs space... he loves me... she's nothing, it's nothing... it's all nothing. I don't love him. All those times and I believed him – he was too drunk to drive, he was staying at a friend's. I trusted him, I cared. I don't want to cry, I don't know why I'm crying.

JO: Do you still love him?

JULIA: I just want him to fall under a train and lose both his legs.

JO: You'd have to look after him then. What's his name?

JULIA: Leonard.

JO: Lenny.

JULIA: Leonard.

JO: I had a boyfriend called Lenny.

JULIA: You won't tell my mum.

JO: Lenny.

JULIA: Please don't tell my mum.

Enter PAUL. Gets under sleeping bag on sofa.

JO: He was doing an advanced diploma in Creative Theatre and Puppetry – he's very talented. They did this big celebration in Peckham with giant puppets – I helped make a dragon and he ran off to Brixton with the designer. I think they're going to do something there next, he's really into African culture.

JULIA: You won't tell my mum.

JO: No. Are your children black?

JULIA: Yes, they're black.

JO: I'm an Anarcho-syndicalist.

JULIA: Are your parents white?

JO: Yeah but my mother's side are Irish.

JULIA: Do you really believe the world is going to end in fifty years?

JO: Yeah. The planet's had enough.

PAUL: It's all over, finished, it'll take another war to put things right.

JO: Did you fight in the war?

PAUL: No. I had to wear hobnail boots that were too small for me eat, tripe and live on a farm in Wales. I was happy as a pig in shit. I've been unhappy ever since.

Enter JOHN.

That's the last time I'm sleeping with you, you kept your trousers on all night.

JOHN: It didn't feel right taking them off.

PAUL: Why, what did you think I was going to do?

JOHN: Nothing, I thought I was at home.

PAUL: Well don't do it again.

JOHN: I was drunk. So were you.

PAUL: I'm the only person allowed to get into my bed with his trousers on.

JOHN: Alright.

PAUL: Right.

JOHN: You should've seen him girls. He was magnificent. What a voice. You can throw all those pills out now. We spent all night down the pub. It was Karaoke night. There was no stopping him.

PAUL: I don't feel well.

JOHN: That's just the hangover.

PAUL: I'm dying.

JOHN: We'll soon have you back on the road – we'll get a really cushy number, like driving a bunch of soft students round Europe.

PAUL: I'm never going out again.

PAUL pulls sleeping bag over his head.

JOHN: Bloody hell.

JULIA offers JO a cigarette.

JO: No thanks, I don't smoke cigarettes.

JULIA lights up. Enter MARY with a hoover. Exit JULIA.

JOHN: Ah, Mary.

MARY: You'll all have to move.

JOHN: You missed a good night last night Mary.

MARY: I've got to hoover.

JO: I'm waiting for Colin.

MARY: Lucky Colin.

Enter JULIA smoking with ashtray.

JULIA: I've locked myself out at home, I'll have to stay with you another night.

MARY hoovers. MARY stops hoovering.

MARY: Since when have you smoked. You don't smoke.

JULIA: I've started.

MARY: Don't be stupid.

JOHN: Listen.

JULIA: I need a cigarette.

JOHN: Listen will you.

MARY: You'll kill yourself.

JOHN: Listen.

MARY: What?

Silence.

JOHN: It's stopped raining.

MARY: Go on then, kill yourself.

JULIA: You don't care.

MARY: You don't care.

JULIA: You don't care.

MARY: You don't care.

JO: I'll wait upstairs.

Exit JO.

JOHN: A circus acrobat fell a hundred and fifty foot to his death the other day, in front of a live audience in Chichester.

MARY: When.

JOHN: The other day.

MARY: I had a feeling something like that was going to happen.

JOHN: You knew it was going to happen?

MARY: I had this feeling the other day.

JOHN: You should have told somebody in Chichester.

MARY: Just move will you.

Exit JOHN. MARY hoovers.

PAUL: Right!

PAUL throws back his sleeping bag and storms out the room. MARY stops hoovering.

MARY: Whose keys are those?

JULIA: I don't know.

MARY: How did they get there?

JULIA: I don't know. They were in the front door.

MARY picks up the keys.

MARY: He's been out. He's been to the off licence again, I knew there was something wrong by the state of his feet – I've told them not to serve him, they don't listen, nobody listens. He can go to the pub for the night, he goes to the off licence, he can do his own shopping.

MARY hoovers. She stops.

Please don't smoke, you'll kill yourself. There's something going on, what's going on?

JULIA: Nothing.

MARY: What's wrong?

JULIA: Nothing's wrong.

MARY: How was your husband.

JULIA: I don't know, I didn't see him – I've lost my keys, I've locked myself out... I rang him at work but he wasn't there – the children are at his mother's.

MARY: So everything's alright, it's all alright. Alright, don't tell me, what do I care, I'm your mother – my mother didn't speak to me for five years after I married your father, she said to me, "Expect nothing but pain from your children and you'll never be disappointed".

MARY bends to pick up hoover, drops it and remains bent over.

JULIA: What, what is it what's the matter?

MARY: I can't move.

JULIA: What's wrong?

MARY: I can't move.

JULIA: Lie down.

MARY: It's my back.

JULIA: Lie down on the floor.

MARY: I can't move.

JULIA: I'll ring for a doctor.

MARY: No don't.

JULIA: You can't move.

MARY: I don't want a doctor.

JULIA: You need a doctor.

MARY: Don't shout at me.

JULIA: I'm not shouting.

MARY: I'll be alright, I don't want a doctor, don't call a doctor.

MARY slowly lowers herself to the floor. JULIA goes to help her.

No, I'm alright – I can manage, it'll go away, it's nothing, I'm alright.

MARY rolls onto her back, knees in the air.

It's nothing.

JULIA: It might be serious.

MARY: How do you know?

JULIA: No, no it's not serious.

MARY: How do you know it's not serious?

JULIA: It's not serious.

MARY: It's my nerves, I've got bad nerves, that's all – stop fussing will you.

JULIA: I'm not fussing.

MARY: I'm alright, I can manage.

JULIA: I'll get some deep heat.

MARY: Where did you get those boots from.

JULIA: What's wrong with my boots?

MARY: Nothing.

JULIA: I like them.

MARY: They don't do anything for your legs.

JULIA: I'll get some deep heat.

MARY: You look like a tart.

JULIA: I like them, I bought them for me I didn't buy them for you. I knew you wouldn't like them.

MARY: That's why you bought them.

JULIA: I bought them because I feel small.

MARY: You're not small, you've got big bones.

JULIA: I feel small.

MARY: You could do with putting some weight on, you don't need shoes for that.

JULIA: All the time I was buying them you were there, a small nagging voice – I can't even buy a stick of lipstick without feeling bad. I had to pretend they weren't for me – I said I was an actress and I needed them for a musical I was in – the woman in the shop wanted to know what musical and I wanted to die, and I said it's a musical about a man who loses both his legs in a car crash and I have to sing and dance in it, she said she'd never heard of it and asked if she could come and see it and what was it called – so I said "Lost in Lagos" – took the boots and ran out the shop.

MARY: Why Lagos.

JULIA: I didn't even try them on.

MARY: They're common.

JULIA: I like them.

MARY: I wouldn't be seen dead in them.

JULIA: Don't wear them then.

MARY: I'm only speaking my mind. You do you look common.

Exit JULIA.

Oh Julia... Julia... Julia!

Scene 8

JOHN on the phone.

JOHN: Hello, Doreen, Doreen sugar... anyone there, it's me... Oh well, I miss you sugar, bye.

Dials again. Enter PAUL with a bottle of whisky.

The wife.

PAUL: I'm making a cup of cocoa.

Exit PAUL.

JOHN: Hello sugar... Oh, hello, I'd like to speak to Joyce please – oh, she's out – A friend, who are you?... no, no message.

Dials again.

JOHN: Hello, Rita, it's me sugar... are you there sugar – I know you're there sugar, I miss you sugar, I love you sugar – pick up the phone sugar ...

JOHN slams down the phone. Enter PAUL with a mug.

PAUL: It's cocoa. I made a cup of cocoa. You look like you could do with a cup of cocoa.

JOHN: Yeah.

PAUL: Mary and Julia are stopping over. They're in the box-room. Mary's on the floor. It's her back. You can come in with me.

JOHN: Yeah.

PAUL: Night then.

JOHN: Night.

Exit PAUL. JOHN puts on 'Always On My Mind' sung by Elvis Presley and lights a cigarette.

Scene 9

REG and RALPH. A bottle of wine and beer.

REG: Please make me suck your cock.

RALPH: No.

REG: Please make me suck your cock.

RALPH: You don't mean it.

REG: I do – look, do I have to?

RALPH: Yes.

REG: I can't.

RALPH: Yes you can. Go on – say it.

REG: Please make me suck your cock.

RALPH: No. What is it?

REG: I can't.

RALPH: You can – What is it?

REG: A cock.

JO laughs offstage.

JO: (*Offstage.*) No – no.

REG: A big cock.

RALPH: Yes.

REG: Yeah.

RALPH: Say it.

REG: Big cock.

RALPH: Say big.

REG: Big.

RALPH: Say cock.

REG: Cock.

RALPH: Say it.

REG: Big cock.

RALPH: Now say it again.

REG: Please make me suck your cock.

RALPH: Yes!

JO laughs offstage.

JO: (*Offstage.*) Colin.

REG: And then what would she say?

RALPH: She wouldn't say anything.

REG: Then what? Go on. Go on. Oh, alright.

RALPH: And then she gags on it.

REG: Yeah.

RALPH: Yeah. And then I take it out and she can't take her eyes off it, she can't believe it.

REG: What does she say?

RALPH: She doesn't say anything, she just looks up and I'm looking down and I'm saying – "Yeah you're right, it is". And then I say, "Bend over I'm going to give it you straight up the middle."

REG: And then what?

RALPH: And then I give it her... inch by inch ...

REG: What about her?

RALPH: She says, "Give it me, all of it, as much as I can take."

REG: Yeah.

RALPH: Yeah. And then I give her the rest of it.

JO: (*Offstage.*) No, Colin, don't.

Loud scream of laughter and running.

REG: And then what does she say?

RALPH: She wouldn't say anything. I'd just do unspeakably dirty things to her.

REG: Ah don't stop there. Go on. You're good at stories you.

RALPH: No. You go on.

REG: I can't. I'm no good at stories.

COLIN appears in the doorway. He doesn't enter the room. He smiles.

COLIN: Uh – ooh – ooh – ooh – ooh!

COLIN imitates an ape and disappears. RALPH covers his face with his hands and distorts his features.

RALPH: Ohhhhh.

REG: What's the matter?

RALPH: Nothing.

REG: You don't look well.

RALPH: I'm not – I feel bad, really bad, terrible, awful, bad all over.

REG: What is it?

RALPH: I don't know.

REG: You should see a doctor.

RALPH: Yeah.

REG: Here, have a drink.

RALPH: I've got wine thanks.

REG: Don't be soft.

REG gives RALPH his beer.

Go on, drink it.

RALPH: I don't like Newcastle Brown.

REG: It's good for you. Go on.

RALPH: Do I have to?

REG: Yes.

> *RALPH drinks. Puts bottle down.*

All of it, or it doesn't work.

> *RALPH finishes bottle.*

RALPH: Thanks.

REG: I followed this girl off the bus the other day – so high, blonde, blue eyes, leather jacket, loads of make up, I couldn't take my eyes off her.

RALPH: Go on – what's she look like?

REG: Blonde. I followed her all the way to Victoria station, right onto the platform.

RALPH: Yeah?

REG: Yeah.

RALPH: And then what?

REG: She got a train to East Grinstead.

> *RALPH smothers his face with his hands.*

RALPH: Ohhhhh.

REG: Have another bottle if you like.

> *Noise from above of people and furniture falling over. JO laughs offstage. Enter JULIA in a man's dressing gown.*

JULIA: I can't sleep.

RALPH: We're having a party.

> *Exit JULIA.*

The dark deep continent of Africa.

REG: Here, have you?

RALPH: What? No.

REG: Me neither.

RALPH: Africa.

REG: She's nice.

Enter JULIA.

RALPH: We were just talking about Africa.

JULIA: Oh.

REG: You've got a glass of water.

JULIA: I've never been.

REG: Neither have we.

RALPH: We were thinking of going.

REG: How's Mary?

JULIA: Alright.

REG: How's her back.

RALPH: You're stopping overnight then.

JULIA: She's sleeping on the floor.

RALPH: Where are you sleeping?

JULIA: We're in the spare room.

RALPH: I'd like to go to Africa, wouldn't we Reg.

JULIA: What for?

REG: Well, it's big –

RALPH: Yeah, very big.

REG: I'll get some beer.

Exit REG.

JO: (*Offstage.*) I mean it Colin... I will... I will ...

COLIN: (*Offstage.*) Arrrgh.

RALPH: Have you seen Reservoir Dogs?

JULIA: No.

RALPH: I hate sentimentality.

Enter REG with beer.

REG: Here we go then.

REG offers JULIA a beer.

JULIA: No thanks.

RALPH: Have a drink.

JULIA: I've got water.

RALPH: Have a glass of wine.

> *RALPH pours her a large glass of wine. She takes it and drinks it in one.*

REG: Cheers.

RALPH: Cheers.

> *RALPH pours her another large glass. She drinks it. RALPH tips glass of wine over his head.*

Whey-hey! I'm mad me, mad, mad, mad. Do you like musicals?

JULIA: No.

RALPH: Me neither – I was in West Side Story at school, we had a progressive English teacher, I was a Jet – (*Sings.*) "When you're a Jet you're a Jet all the way from your first cigarette..."

COLIN: (*Offstage.*) Give them here will you.

RALPH: Reg mate –

JO: (*Offstage.*) No.

RALPH: I love you – I love you, this boy's magic. I fancied the English teacher.

JULIA: I'll go back to bed then.

REG: No, don't go.

> *Enter JO with COLIN's trousers chased by COLIN.*

COLIN: Oh, you're still up then.

JULIA: I couldn't sleep.

COLIN: Yeah, summer and it pisses down with rain.

JO: I love thunderstorms.

COLIN: Yeah.

JULIA: Goodnight then.

RALPH: Oh, don't go.

REG: No, don't go – you can sleep in my bed.

COLIN: Oh, aye.

REG: I'll sleep down here.

RALPH: You haven't got any trousers on.

COLIN: I don't like trousers, I never have.

JO: It's only a bit of fun.

REG: It's no bother, honest.

COLIN: You can have my bed if you like Ralph.

RALPH: No thanks.

COLIN: Come on, let's party – here listen to this, you'll like this – one of John's.

Puts on tape. 'Houndog' by Elvis Presley.

JO: Yeah.

She dances.

COLIN: Yeah.

He turns up the volume and dances with JO. REG goes to dance with JULIA.

JULIA: No, I can't.

REG pulls her into dance. They dance. Exit RALPH. COLIN, JO, REG and JULIA dance. Enter JOHN in pyjamas. He turns off the music.

JOHN: Some of us are trying to sleep. Show some bloody respect will you.

Exit JOHN.

JO: I want to do what they do in that film – drive through the desert, in a big flash open top American car at night – stop, turn up the music, and dance like crazy in the headlights.

COLIN: (*American accent.*) Come on baby, let's do it.

JO: Yeah.

COLIN: See you in the morning then.

Exit COLIN and JO.

REG: You look nice like that.

JULIA: It's your dad's.

REG: I know.

JULIA: Goodnight then.

REG: Yeah, goodnight.

JULIA: It's late. It's gone five.

REG kisses JULIA. They kiss. She breaks away.

I can't.

Exit JULIA. REG lies down on the sofa and goes to sleep.

Scene 10

The following morning. REG asleep on the sofa. Enter PAUL. He goes to lie on the sofa. Enter COLIN.

COLIN: Morning Pops, I'm making a cup of tea, do you want one?

PAUL: Bloody cheek.

COLIN: Yeah – pot's brewed.

PAUL: Bloody nerve.

COLIN: You're not dead yet then dad. Well do you?

PAUL: What?

COLIN: Want a cup of tea.

PAUL: Do my leg will you, I'm seizing up, my whole body is seizing up.

COLIN: Someone got lucky last night, grandad.

PAUL: I'm not your grandad.

COLIN: You're not my dad either – when my mam got your letter she didn't know who you were.

PAUL: She was the only one to answer. Reggie's mum died.

COLIN: My mam doesn't know you.

PAUL: I loved your mother.

COLIN: Are you calling my mam a liar?

Exit COLIN. PAUL takes out a packet of photos and spreads them out on the table and admires them. Enter COLIN with two cups of tea.

PAUL: I wanted lemon in mine.

COLIN: They're not for you.

PAUL: Pull my arm.

COLIN sees the photographs.

COLIN: Here, they're all naked.

PAUL: I loved them all.

COLIN: You could get some of these on the readers' wives page.

PAUL: I love women – that's my trouble, I love them too much.

COLIN picks up a photograph. Enter JOHN.

Oh yes. Beautiful. Beautiful dark brown nipples, cooked a lovely hotpot with swimmers.

COLIN: Swimmers?

PAUL: Dumplings.

COLIN: She can't cook.

PAUL: Whose hotpot was it then?

COLIN: You talk about my mam like that again and I'll kill you.

PAUL: I'm sorry son, I didn't mean to insult your mother's cooking.

COLIN: I don't want your money, right, I don't want anything.

COLIN pockets the photo.

PAUL: That's my photograph.

COLIN: She's my mam.

Exit COLIN.

PAUL: Do my leg will you. I'm dying.

JOHN: No you're not.

PAUL: I'm dying. I woke up this morning and I didn't know who I was... I thought I was going to be fifty and then I remembered.

JOHN: Look, can I have a word.

PAUL: I can't taste anything.

JOHN: It won't take long.

PAUL: I've lost everything.

JOHN: You're not old. It's the wife... she's found out. Look, I'm not on holiday. They gave me the sack, three weeks ago I turned up to the yard and they gave me my cards.

PAUL: What about the coach?

JOHN: I just took it and came here. I told the wife I told them all that I was doing a tour of Scotland, that I'd be back in two weeks. So it's gone two weeks and I'm still not back and the wife rings the yard, and she says she's my wife and she's looking for me. And there's this new girl on the switchboard and she says, "How many wives has this John got, you're the third this week and anyway he doesn't work here anymore, and if you see him we want the coach back, or it'll be a matter for the police". I keep having these dreams.

PAUL: Yes.

JOHN: Last night I dreamt about the Broadway Steak Bar.

PAUL: What, in Cardiff.?

JOHN: Yeah.

PAUL: I always had a mixed grill in Cardiff.

JOHN: Everything was for free and I couldn't get in.

PAUL: I always had to undo my belt when we went to the Broadway Steak Bar.

JOHN: It's over.

JOHN takes out his wallet and shows PAUL three photographs. REG wakes up.

Beautiful aren't they.

PAUL: You married them all?

JOHN: No, just Rita – I would've if I could, but I couldn't. I love her, I love them all.

REG: Morning John, how's the bus.

Enter JULIA followed by MARY.

MARY: So what did you do?

JULIA: I was tired.

MARY: So you slept all night?

REG: Would you like some coffee?

MARY: (*Together.*) No.

JULIA: (*Together.*) Yes.

MARY: So you slept. You didn't come back to bed.

JULIA: I felt sick, I had a drink, I don't remember, I went out.

MARY: What time?

JULIA: I don't know.

MARY: Your bed was empty all night.

JULIA: I went for a walk, I'm twenty seven, I had a drink.

MARY: You were drunk. You're just like your father. Where were you?

JOHN: I think I can help here Mary.

MARY: Oh, shut up will you.

PAUL: Yes, shut up.

MARY: Have you taken your tablet?

PAUL: No.

MARY: Well go and take it then. You got up and didn't come back to bed.

JULIA: I went to a friend's. Don't.

MARY: So, you've got a friend.

JULIA: Please, don't.

MARY: You walked to a friend's. It rained.

JULIA: I don't remember.

MARY: I couldn't sleep, your bed was empty, I was in pain. Loud music and laughing downstairs. You didn't come back. So, you've got a friend. That's nice, was it nice, did you have a good time?

JULIA: I feel sick.

MARY: Tell me.

JULIA: I went to a friend's.

MARY: What did you do?

JULIA: We talked.

MARY: Oh that's nice, you've got a friend, you walked in the rain, you talked. Why can't you tell me, just tell me the truth.

JULIA: Alright. I stayed up, I had a drink, we had a dance, I didn't come back to bed, I slept in Reg's bed.

MARY: You're a married woman.

JULIA: So?

MARY: (*To REG.*) Was it good?

REG: What?

JULIA: Yes!

REG: Nothing happened.

JULIA: I'm just like my mother, I can't help it.

MARY slaps JULIA across the face.

MARY: Slut – tramp – black trash.

JOHN: You, outside now.

REG: Mary.

JOHN: I said outside.

REG: Nothing happened.

JOHN: Don't take the piss with me son.

REG: I'm not.

JOHN: You've been taking the piss ever since I got here.

REG: So what are you going to do about it?

PAUL: Pack it in the pair of you.

JOHN: No, he's been asking for it. Don't you worry Mary, I'll sort this out I was in the merchant navy for five years. Come on then. See what you've done – happy eh – a good woman like that.

REG goes for JOHN but PAUL gets in the way and keeps them apart.

PAUL: Now pack it in. All of you. This is my house. I won't have it, none of it, pack it in, the lot of you. This is my house. I won't have any of it. You hear. This is my house.

Exit PAUL.

JOHN: It's a good job I'm a friend of your dad's. You should be ashamed of yourself, she's a married woman – it's disgusting.

Exit JOHN.

REG: If there's anything you need... if you need anything.

Exit REG. MARY near to tears.

MARY: They should have dropped the bomb while they had the chance.

JULIA: Mum. Please. Don't. It's alright, I'm alright, we're alright.

MARY: Why won't you tell me.

JULIA: What. Tell you what.

MARY: If your father wasn't dead already I'd kill him. We'd manage alright, it didn't matter... All these years, everyday I've died... the looks, the look of mothers, the look of judgement. And not one of them has the nerve, it's written all over their faces... no one says anything.

I feel so small I collapse and disappear. I can't just say, he let me down. He let me down. Anyone asks, he was a wonderful man, everyone loved him. I loved him. He was always cheating, always lying, always down the Afro-Carribean carrying on... he said he loved me, he was never there. Somebody showed me love and I took it... your father tried to kill me – I ran for my life... And now it's happening all over again. I did nothing wrong, I've got nothing to be ashamed of.

Scene 11

Enter JO followed closely by RALPH.

JO: I don't want to.

RALPH: Come on.

She pushes him away.

JO: I said no. It's over between us.

RALPH: So – what's that got to do with it.

He pulls her to him and gyrates.

JO: Get off.

RALPH: What, because of Colin?

JO: No.

RALPH: Then what?

JO: I don't like you.

RALPH: I don't like you.

JO: I don't like you.

RALPH: I don't like you.

JO: I don't like you.

RALPH kisses JO.

Stop it.

RALPH: You like it.

JO: No I don't.

RALPH: You do.

JO: I don't like you.

RALPH: Yeah, but we have great sex.

JO: No, I can't. I'll go and get Paul for you.

RALPH: So, you've moved in.

JO: No.

RALPH: I've missed you. I have.

JO: I've been here.

RALPH: I've missed you. Honest. What, what are you smiling at?

JO: Nothing.

RALPH: You smiled.

JO: No I didn't.

RALPH: I've missed you, I have.

JO: Is that why you're here?

RALPH: Yeah.

JO: Liar.

RALPH: No I'm not.

JO: So why do you want to see Paul?

RALPH: I don't. It's business.

JO: I'll go and get him for you.

RALPH: Come on.

JO: No.

RALPH: So you're fucking Colin.

JO: That's got nothing to do with you.

RALPH: Alright, so you're making love to him – you don't have sex with Colin, you make love.

JO: Colin's got nothing to do with it. That's different.

RALPH: Come on.

JO: We don't get on.

RALPH: You like it with me, you know you do.

JO: No.

RALPH: Come on.

JO: I can't. I just can't sleep with two people at the same time.

RALPH: Of course you can.

JO: It'll do my head in.

RALPH: Look at it like this – you can have sex with me and make love to Colin – get the best of both worlds.

JO: What about Colin?

RALPH: What about him.

JO: He's got feelings as well you know.

RALPH: So don't tell me Colin's got nothing to do with it – I can't fuck you because Colin's got feelings – if Colin's got nothing to do with it then it doesn't matter – if I've got nothing to do with what goes on between you and him, then he's got nothing to do with what goes on between you and me, so let's have a fuck.

JO: Don't try and confuse me.

RALPH: You confused – it's me that's confused.

JO: I love him.

RALPH: Oh, grow up.

JO: Fuck off Ralph.

RALPH: You want me to fuck off?

JO: Yeah?

RALPH: Yeah.

JO: Yes.

RALPH: I'll fuck off then – after all I've done for you.

JO: What have you done for me?

RALPH: If you don't know, I'm not telling you.

JO: Ralph.

RALPH: No, sorry, I can't talk to you – it wouldn't be right – Colin's got feelings as well you know, how would he like it me talking to you.

JO: Please don't.

RALPH: What?

JO: All this.

RALPH: All what?

JO: I don't want it to end like this, I want us to be friends.

RALPH: I know what I want, I want... you want love, an all consuming burning passion – it doesn't bother me, you and Colin, it's just sad, something to be pitied, I don't envy you at all.

Enter JOHN and PAUL. PAUL in blazer and trousers.

PAUL: Come on.

JOHN: I don't want to get caught in traffic.

PAUL: You wont.

JOHN: I hate the North Circular.

PAUL: Don't take it then. Ah, Ralph, what do you think?

RALPH: Yeah, great.

Exit RALPH.

PAUL: What's the matter with him?

JO: Why ask me, don't ask me, ask him, how should I know?

Exit JO.

JOHN: What's the matter with her?

PAUL: Don't ask me, ask her, how should I know?

JOHN: I hate the North Circular.

PAUL: Well don't take it.

JOHN: No, I won't.

PAUL: Come on, up against the wall.

They push the sofa against the wall.

The other way up, upside down. I'm not lying down again.

JOHN: You can't not lie down.

PAUL: I don't want to lie down.

JOHN: Alright.

They tip the sofa upside down.

She's not here.

PAUL: (*Pulls stomach in.*) It used to be like an ironing board.

JOHN: Maybe she's forgot.

PAUL: She'll be here. A steel ironing board.

JOHN: Oh, yeah?

PAUL: You've never known what it's like to be healthy.

JOHN: I'm not waiting all day.

PAUL: She'll be here. I never used to be fat.

JOHN: You're not fat.

PAUL: I can't do up the button.

JOHN: It looks better that way.

PAUL: You think so?

JOHN: Tidy but casual.

PAUL: You're just saying that.

JOHN: No, I'm not – a real ladykiller.

PAUL: Stop taking the piss.

JOHN: I'm not.

PAUL: I'm going to get into shape. What's it like out?

JOHN: Hot.

PAUL: I won't be too hot?

JOHN: No. She's not coming.

PAUL: It's alright out?

JOHN: Yes.

PAUL: Give us a fag. Go on.

JOHN: You've given up.

PAUL: Tomorrow. Go on, just the one.

JOHN gives PAUL a cigarette.

Ta. John Paul Coaches.

JOHN: We haven't got the money.

PAUL: We've got something more valuable. Experience. You can't buy that, you can't put a price on experience. It's worth more than money. I'll go and see the bank manager tomorrow and see what he says, they give loans to people like us. All we've got to do is look out for each other.

JOHN: You're not well.

PAUL: I'm fit enough.

JOHN: You're not up to it.

PAUL: It's all in the mind son – all I have to do is cut out the drink and... keep taking the tablets. You don't want to?

JOHN: I never said that.

PAUL: You don't think I'm up to it? Look, if I can't make it further than the end of the road you can always bring me back and we'll try again tomorrow. You'll see I'm alright.

JOHN: Yeah.

PAUL: John Paul Tours.

JOHN: How come my name gets to go first?

PAUL: What's in a name?

PAUL coughs.

JOHN: Here.

Takes PAUL's cigarette.

PAUL: No, don't.

JOHN: You want to stop this for a start.

PAUL: I am – tomorrow.

JOHN stubs out cigarette.

What did you do that for?

JOHN: It's killing you.

PAUL: I was enjoying that.

> *PAUL takes JOHN's fag and stubs it out.*

JOHN: What d'you do that for?

PAUL: It's killing you.

JOHN: I'm not the one that's sick.

PAUL: We'll use your redundancy as collateral.

JOHN: What about yours?

PAUL: John Paul Tours.

JOHN: We could specialise in trips to the Vatican.

PAUL: Now you're thinking.

> *Enter REG.*

REG: Here, have you seen this phone bill – eight hundred and fifty three pounds and twenty six pence.

> *REG looks at sofa.*

PAUL: I'm throwing it out, it's had it.

REG: Who's died?

PAUL: Don't play silly buggers with me son.

REG: It's not right, there's been a mistake, look all these 01-0852-172 numbers – nearly eight hundred pounds' worth – it's not right.

PAUL: I know.

JOHN: Come on, let's get going.

PAUL: We can't.

JOHN: The'll have me if I don't get the coach back.

> *Enter RALPH.*

RALPH: Ah, Paul, Paul.

> *RALPH puts his arm around PAUL's shoulder and takes him to one side.*

PAUL: You don't look well son.

RALPH: Just a touch of flu that's all.

REG: You're going then.

JOHN: Yes. We're giving Julia a lift home.

REG: Do you have a conductor on your bus or what.

PAUL pulls away from RALPH.

PAUL: I don't want to catch anything infectious.

RALPH: Oh, don't worry about me, it's past the infectious stage.

RALPH draws PAUL close.

REG: I'm going to miss you.

JOHN: If you see Julia, tell her we're waiting.

REG: Right, I'll send her down the bus stop.

JOHN: You won't know what hit you, you'll be horizontal, you'll feel so bad you'll wish you were dead.

REG: Oh, yeah?

JOHN: Yeah.

Exit JOHN. Doorbell rings. Silence.

PAUL: There's someone at the door.

REG: So what?

PAUL: Be a good lad and get it will you.

RALPH: Yeah, get the door Reg.

Exit REG.

PAUL: What about the gas and electric?

RALPH: I'll see to those.

PAUL: So, what do I have to pay for?

RALPH: Just the phone.

PAUL: Oh. You couldn't see your way clear to this quarter could you?

RALPH: Alright, the gas the electric and this quarter's phone bill.

PAUL: And the house is mine?

RALPH: I'll only take possession when you're dead. We'll sign an agreement.

PAUL: It's a pleasure doing business with you son.

RALPH: The pleasure's all mine mate.

They shake hands.

Let's just keep this between you and me. Oooooh!

PAUL: You want to take something for that.

Enter COLIN and JO.

COLIN: We're going to Paris.

JO: Yeah.

PAUL: Here, you don't fancy investing in the travel business as well do you?

Enter REG.

COLIN: (*Hitches up trousers.*) What do you think, eh?

PAUL: Right, anybody wants me I'm sat on John's coach. We're waiting for Julia.

COLIN: Big new fuck off boots.

Exit PAUL.

REG: Where are you going?

JO: Paris.

RALPH: I hate the French.

REG gives COLIN fifty pounds.

COLIN: What's this?

REG: You'll need money.

COLIN: We've got money.

REG: Go on take it.

COLIN: I don't want your money.

REG: It's not my money it's your money – Fat Vincent finally paid Ralph.

RALPH: Yeah.

COLIN: Oh, right. Cheers mate. This must be my lucky day. No hard feelings like?

RALPH: No.

COLIN: Right.

REG: Right.

COLIN: We'll be going then.

REG: Send us a postcard.

COLIN: Yeah.

JO: Yeah.

RALPH: Have a cigar, enjoy yourself mate.

RALPH gives COLIN a cigar.

COLIN: Thanks.

Exit COLIN and JO.

REG: So, what did he say about the house?

RALPH: I don't think he's interested. Who was that at the door?

REG: Life insurance.

RALPH: Ooooh.

REG: It's probably something you ate.

RALPH: Yeah.

Enter JULIA with suitcase.

They're waiting on the coach.

Exit RALPH.

REG: You're all packed then.

JULIA: Have you seen Mary?

REG: About the other night... you haven't made any international calls have you?

JULIA: No.

REG: This bill's not right. I'll maybe see you round then.

Enter MARY.

Now then Mary.

She looks at sofa.

He's throwing it out.

Exit REG.

JULIA: I've arranged to pick up the kids from school. They're waiting on the coach.

MARY gives JULIA a fiver.

MARY: For the children.

JULIA: I'll tell Raffi and Jade you send your love.

MARY: Why couldn't you have given them proper names. What chance have they got with names like that.

Blast of coach horn.

JULIA: You won't forget to ring?

MARY: Ring me when you get home.

JULIA: You'll ring me. I don't want to be late. I'm picking the kids up. I have to pick up the children. I can't stay.

MARY: No, you've got to pick up the children.

JULIA: I do.

MARY: I know you've said.

MARY hugs JULIA. Enter JOHN. MARY breaks the embrace.

JOHN: Come on, or we'll get stuck in traffic.

MARY gives JULIA a handkerchief; JULIA takes it.

MARY: Blow your nose.

JULIA picks up suitcase.

JOHN: I'll take that.

MARY: Next time bring the children.

JULIA: I'll ring, when I get home.

Exit JULIA.

JOHN: The young – they've got it all, the future's down to the young... a hundred years from now we'll have evolved into a new species. How's your knee? We'll get stuck in traffic. If ever you fancy a drink... you could have a bitter lemon or something.

MARY: Yes.

JOHN: Right.

MARY: You'll get stuck in traffic.

JOHN: Yeah.

Exit JOHN. Enter REG and RALPH. Exit MARY.

RALPH: I just need to lie down.

REG helps RALPH pull the sofa out and turn it upright.

I've got some stuff needs delivering.

RALPH lies down on the sofa.

Oh, that's better... my arm... give my arm a pull.

REG pulls RALPH's arm.

Not so hard will you. Where are you going?

REG: Out.

RALPH: No, don't go. I'm not well, I don't feel well, I feel bad... something bad, something really bad's going to happen, I know it is – and I don't know what – I don't know how I got here, one minute I'm standing and the next – just this lacerating pain – up here – you know and nothing makes sense anymore, there's no sense, you don't know who you are or what anything means – it all gets twisted... somebody... something's out to get you...

Exit REG.

There is no point... what's the point – there is only one point... Reg – Reg – Reg!

Enter REG with a glass of water.

Reg. I thought you'd gone.

REG: I am.

RALPH: No, don't go.

REG puts water by RALPH.

Where are you going?

REG: I don't know.

Enter PAUL.

PAUL: I forgot my tablets. Where are my tablets.

Exit PAUL.

RALPH: Don't go.

REG: No, alright.

REG sits. Enter MARY with coat on and a broom. MARY shakes the broom. REG jumps out of his seat.

MARY: This handle's coming loose. Stupid boy.

Enter PAUL with small bottle.

I thought you'd gone.

PAUL: I am.

MARY: What's that?

PAUL: A drop of whisky. For my stomach. For the journey.

MARY: I'm going home.

Silence.

PAUL: I'll have to get that crack in the ceiling fixed. And painted.

MARY: The whole place needs painting.

RALPH turns on the sofa.

RALPH: Oooh.

PAUL: What's the matter with him.

REG: Something he ate.

JOHN: (*Offstage.*) Paul!

PAUL: I'll paint the walls. What colour should I paint the walls?

JOHN: (*Offstage.*) Paul.

MARY: They'll go without you.

PAUL: Right. I'll paint the house.

MARY: You need a new broom.

Exit PAUL and MARY.

RALPH: They've gone.

REG: Yeah. I got you a glass of water.

Exit REG. Silence. RALPH gets out a mobile phone and dials.

RALPH: Hello... yes I'd like to book an appointment... Flynn, captain Flynn – I'm a pilot, a jet fighter pilot... an hour in the fantasy room, with Raquel... no, just me... Friday, seven thirty... cash.

Puts phone down.

Yeah. Oh, my stomach.

Turns over and goes to sleep.

THE END

WASTED

Characters

JOHN
RAY
SHARON
FRAN
NEIL
CAROL
KENNY
MICHAEL

The play is set in the present and takes place in and around a large house in North London. In the garden is an old van which Kenny fixes during the play.

Wasted was first performed by the London Theatre Company at the Old Red Lion Theatre, London, on the 5th of October 1993, with the following cast:

JOHN, Carl Brincat
RAY, Tom Hudson
SHARON, Samantha Edmonds
FRAN, Georgiana Dacombe
NEIL, Mark Powley
CAROL, Rebecca Clay
KENNY, Philip Brook
MICHAEL, Colin Jarrett

DIRECTION: Christopher Hynes
DESIGN: Andrew Hall
LIGHTING DESIGN: Paule Constable
PRODUCED by Howard Slone and Charlotte Barslund

ACT ONE

Scene 1

Kitchen. JOHN in bath towel round his waist. Head over a bowl. He spits into the bowl several times. Enter RAY.

RAY: What you doing?

JOHN: Having a bath.

RAY: You'll have a long wait then, she's in there with two of her mates again. Good night eh?

JOHN: Get us a whisky will you.

RAY: Why?

JOHN: I want a whisky.

RAY: What's the matter?

JOHN: Nothing's the matter.

RAY: You look sick.

JOHN: I feel sick, alright, I feel really bad – like I've done something and I don't know what and I'm paying for it, so just get us a whisky will you.

RAY: Why – what is it you think you've done?

JOHN: Nothing.

RAY: What you feeling bad for then?

JOHN: I don't know.

RAY: You must've done something.

JOHN: I haven't done anything alright.

RAY: Alright.

RAY takes out Mars bar.

Want a bite? I like Mars bars.

JOHN: Yeah.

RAY: Yeah.

JOHN: Go on, get us a whisky.

RAY: Lend us a fiver.

JOHN: I haven't got any money.

RAY: Get it yourself then.

JOHN: Go on – I'd do it for you.

RAY: Would you?

JOHN: Yeah.

RAY: Did you shag her?

JOHN: Go on.

RAY: I'm having a break. What?

JOHN: You, you look bloody stupid, you are bloody stupid.

RAY: You were all over her.

JOHN: I never touched her.

RAY: Like a dog with a bone, you had your hand up her skirt.

JOHN: I was drunk.

RAY: So did you shag her?

JOHN: What d'you take me for?

RAY: She wouldn't let you.

JOHN: You'd fuck anything you would.

JOHN holds bowl and spits into it rapidly. Enter SHARON.

SHARON: Oh, sorry – I'm looking for Carol.

RAY: Probably still out in the van. I'll be down in a minute.

SHARON: She's not here then?

RAY: No. This is John – he lives here, he's sick.

SHARON: I'll look in the van then.

RAY: Yeah – I'll be out in a minute.

SHARON: Maybe he should try lying down.

Exit SHARON.

JOHN: Stupid cow.

RAY: She was being friendly.

JOHN: Who is she?

RAY: Sharon.

JOHN: Stupid cow.

RAY: There's no need to get like that.

JOHN: Like what?

RAY: I hate it when you get like this.

JOHN: Like what?

RAY: Forget it.

JOHN lights cigarette.

Thought you'd stopped.

JOHN: I have.

RAY: So why you smoking?

JOHN: I want a fag.

RAY: You need to get out that's what you need, get away for the weekend.

JOHN: Alright we'll go away.

RAY: I can't afford to go anywhere. Well I can't.

JOHN: Thought you were going to help Sharon.

RAY: It's raining. You stopping off work then – go for a drink later eh?

JOHN: I'm not drinking.

RAY: You drink too much.

JOHN: I drink too much.

RAY: Yeah, you're going to pot. We could go to Brighton.

JOHN: You haven't got any money.

RAY: Go on your own then.

JOHN: I'm not going to Brighton.

RAY: What's wrong with Brighton?

JOHN: It's full of wankers.

RAY: Where do you like?

JOHN: Nowhere.

RAY: Miserable sod.

JOHN: Bangkok.

RAY: Miserable sod.

JOHN: I'll lend you some money.

RAY: I don't want your money.

JOHN gets up and pours himself a whisky.

Here, if you could shag anyone in the world who would it be? I'd shag Kylie Minogue.

JOHN: Oh yeah?

RAY: Yeah.

JOHN: What if she started to sing?

RAY: She wouldn't get a chance.

JOHN: I'll go on my own then – yeah, somewhere by the sea – book into a bed and breakfast have a few bets, go down the amusement arcades, have a few beers, go to a club, get blind drunk then back to the bed and breakfast and shag someone I don't know.

RAY: There's about six million people round here you don't know, why not shag one of them.

JOHN: Because it wouldn't be the same.

RAY: Cost less.

JOHN: Stay here then.

RAY: I'll sleep in the car.

JOHN: Don't be soft.

RAY: I'm not being soft.

JOHN: You can't sleep in the car.

RAY: Why not?

JOHN: You won't pull anything sleeping in the car.

RAY: I'm not paying for a bed and breakfast.

JOHN: I've said I'll lend you the money.

RAY: I'm not coming if I can't sleep in the car.

JOHN: Alright, do what you want, buy yourself a crate of beer and never get out the bloody car for all I care.

RAY: Great – where we going?

JOHN: Clacton.

RAY: She wouldn't let you, would she?

JOHN: Fuck off.

RAY: That's what all this is about.

JOHN: All what?

RAY: So come on, who would you shag?

Enter FRAN and NEIL.

NEIL: Fran –

FRAN: Just don't.

RAY: I'm off then.

Exit RAY.

FRAN: Keep away from me.

NEIL: But Fran –

FRAN: Don't.

JOHN: Have you finished in the bathroom?

FRAN: No!

JOHN: Great, fuckin' great.

Exit JOHN.

NEIL: Just listen to me will you.

FRAN: I don't care – don't touch me.

NEIL: It's not what you think.

FRAN: What, what do I think, stop telling me what I think will you.

NEIL: She wasn't anybody.

FRAN: Who was she then? She must have been somebody, she knew you alright, a real live doll – you could see the seams.

NEIL: I hardly know her.

FRAN: You gave her my telephone number.

NEIL: No I didn't.

FRAN: So who gave it her?

NEIL: How should I know?

FRAN: Who else do you give my number to?

NEIL: It's not your bloody telephone, there are other people live here you know, you don't own the place – I live here.

FRAN: Because of me.

NEIL: I'm a member of the co-op.

FRAN: Because of me. Anything under twenty five in a mini skirt with a stupid grin on its face, no wonder the phone keeps going.

NEIL: I thought you didn't care anymore.

FRAN: It doesn't mean I have to watch.

NEIL: Look, I don't want to – not with anyone else, alright. I don't.

FRAN: What about her?

NEIL: Who?

FRAN: Nellie.

NEIL: Lottie.

FRAN: She'd have you back, why not go back to her.

NEIL: That's over, finished, I haven't seen her for three years – I don't even know where she lives.

FRAN: Maybe it's her that keeps ringing and hanging up, waiting for you to answer so you can make love to her over the phone – that's what you do isn't it.

NEIL: You what?

FRAN: That's what you told me.

NEIL: When?

FRAN: When you were on tour with that political puppet theatre.

NEIL: I don't remember.

FRAN: They hired you to drive the van.

NEIL: I don't remember saying it to you.

FRAN: There must be something you can take for a memory like that. You just walked back in and took advantage of me, just like everyone else.

NEIL: Who takes advantage of you?

FRAN: Everybody.

NEIL: Who?

FRAN: You, you live here.

NEIL: But what do I do?

FRAN: You tell me.

NEIL: Nothing, I haven't done anything.

FRAN: I don't want to sleep with you Neil.

NEIL: I don't want to sleep with you.

FRAN goes to leave.

No wait –

FRAN: What?

NEIL: I don't know...

FRAN: What?

NEIL: I just wanted to say...

FRAN: What?

FRAN smiles.

It's not funny, I'm not laughing, I don't love you.

NEIL: I don't love you.

FRAN: I don't love you.

NEIL: I don't love you.

FRAN: I don't love you.

Exit FRAN. Exit NEIL. Enter CAROL and SHARON.

CAROL: Well?

SHARON: Yeah.

CAROL: Don't force yourself.

SHARON: Yeah – it's big. What's the garden like?

CAROL: Big.

SHARON: Do they grow vegetables? Looks the sort of place they grow vegetables.

CAROL: So – not a crime is it?

SHARON: D'you all take turns at digging in it?

CAROL: Sharon.

SHARON: Well I don't know do I, I've never lived in a commune.

CAROL: It's not a commune.

SHARON: They haven't got a lock on the bathroom door.

CAROL: You should have knocked.

SHARON: Doesn't bother me, I don't live here.

CAROL: You were nosing.

SHARON: I was just looking, how was I to know they were having an orgy?

CAROL: It wasn't an orgy.

SHARON: So what do you call three in a bath then?

CAROL: I don't know why you bothered coming, all you've done is complain, you haven't lifted a finger to help – just poked your nose in where it didn't belong.

SHARON: I was looking to see if there's a shower.

CAROL: You haven't even made a cup of tea.

SHARON: That's the thanks I get is it?

CAROL: For what?

SHARON: For taking the day off work.

CAROL: It's your day off.

SHARON: So, I didn't have to come here did I.

CAROL: So, I didn't ask you did I.

Enter RAY.

RAY: That's the lot then... it's all up there... wasn't as much stuff as I thought.

SHARON: She hasn't got much.

CAROL: I've got all I need.

SHARON: It's those little vans.

CAROL: Would you like a beer Ray?

SHARON: They're deceptive – they make it look like there's more than there is.

RAY: Thanks.

SHARON: What about me?

CAROL: You don't drink beer.

RAY: Cheers.

SHARON: (*Together.*) Cheers.

CAROL: (*Together.*) Cheers.

RAY: So, where do you live then Sharon?

SHARON: Over by the park.

RAY: Not far eh.

CAROL: I was sleeping on Sharon's floor.

SHARON: You had a lilo.

CAROL: On the floor.

RAY: We'll all have to go out one night – celebrate Carol moving in, go for a pint.

SHARON: I don't drink beer.

RAY: You're from up North then.

CAROL: (*Together.*) Glasgow.

SHARON: (*Together.*) Manchester.

RAY: I like it up North, it's friendly.

SHARON: Yeah.

RAY: I went to Leeds once, very friendly.

SHARON: You should go and live there then.

CAROL: So, what is it you do again Ray?

RAY: Self employed – building trade you know plumbing, electrics – so if there's anything you need fixing just give us a ring – I could come round and fix your meters for you if you like.

SHARON: They're not broke.

RAY: Like paying bills do you?

SHARON: No.

RAY: You don't have to then.

SHARON: You can't just not pay the bills.

RAY: We don't get any.

SHARON: Carol.

CAROL: I'll make some tea.

SHARON: Carol.

CAROL: What?

RAY: So you don't want me to do yours for you?

SHARON: No.

RAY: Suppose you pay for the telly'n'all?

SHARON: It's not right, if you don't pay somebody has to –
so who pays?

RAY: No one it's free – the Gas, the Electricity, they can afford
it.

CAROL: Have another beer Ray, I bought them for you.

RAY takes a beer.

RAY: Bloody rich I hate the parasites.

Exit RAY.

SHARON: They'll have you, I'm telling you, they put people
away for less than that.

CAROL: You can come and visit me then.

SHARON: Well I couldn't live like it.

CAROL: No one's asking you to.

SHARON: No – I don't get asked anything.

CAROL: Stop going on will you.

SHARON: And it's dirty.

CAROL: You sound just like me mam.

SHARON: Well she wouldn't like it either.

CAROL: Shut up will you.

SHARON: I'm only speaking my mind, you wouldn't want me to lie would you?

CAROL: Why not?

SHARON: Right.

CAROL: Right.

SHARON: I'll shut up then. Look, I'm only saying because –

CAROL: I know what you're saying.

SHARON: There's no need to get like that.

CAROL: I'm not getting like anything.

SHARON: They're a bunch of crooks.

CAROL: He was being friendly.

SHARON: Yeah dead friendly, maybe we should all have taken a bath together.

CAROL: Don't start that again.

SHARON: It was an orgy I'm telling you – three of them in a bath – naked, white robes, chanting, throwing petals and splashing water over each other – what else do you call it?

CAROL: Sharon.

SHARON: Alright don't believe me, but I've seen it on the telly, Sex Witches – worse than the Moonies that sort.

CAROL: What sort?

SHARON: Their sort.

CAROL: You don't have to stay you know, nobody's forcing you.

SHARON: I know. What was wrong with my place?

CAROL: Nothing.

SHARON: What was it then?

CAROL: Nothing.

SHARON: So it was me?

CAROL: I didn't say that did I?

SHARON: So what are you saying?

CAROL: Nothing.

SHARON: Go on, say it, I don't mind.

CAROL: Alright –

SHARON: What?

CAROL: It was you.

SHARON: Yeah.

CAROL: Yeah.

Enter FRAN.

FRAN: Oh, Carol – have you seen Neil?

CAROL: No.

FRAN: We're out of sea salt – I forgot – it's my mind, I can't remember anything, sometimes I think I'm going mad – we only need a cup – I don't suppose you bought any with you?

SHARON: What?

FRAN: Sea salt.

CAROL: Oh, no.

FRAN: You're not going anywhere near a shop are you?

CAROL: Well –

FRAN: I'd go myself just – I'm not dressed for it and we've started already.

CAROL: No, no, it's alright, what do you want?

FRAN: You're sure?

CAROL: Yes.

FRAN: I'd get Neil to go but – just some sea salt that's all, there's a shop on the corner does it – don't worry what sort, just say it's for Francesca.

CAROL: Right.

FRAN: So, you're all moved in then.

CAROL: Yeah.

FRAN: I'll cook a meal.

CAROL: This is Sharon – Sharon Fran, Fran Sharon.

SHARON: Sorry about earlier, I didn't know anybody was in there.

FRAN: Oh, that's alright we hadn't got started properly. Look, don't worry if you can't –

CAROL: No – sea salt.

FRAN: You should try it, it's good for the complexion.

SHARON: What do you do, rub it in with soap?

FRAN: Soak in it.

SHARON: I prefer showers.

Exit FRAN.

CAROL: There was no need –

SHARON: Who the hell does she –

Enter FRAN in doorway.

FRAN: And if there's anything you need, just ask, we're in the bathroom.

CAROL: Thanks.

Exit FRAN.

SHARON: Thanks for what?

CAROL: There was no need to be rude.

SHARON: I wasn't. Nosey cow – walking in like that, didn't even knock – the door wasn't open she just –

CAROL: She was being friendly.

SHARON: You're soft you. Hope you've got a lock on your bedroom door – she just wandered in like the place was her own. Women like that they get right up my nose. You won't have any privacy she'll be snooping all the time.

CAROL: Not everyone's like you.

SHARON: What's that mean.

CAROL: You know.

SHARON: No I don't.

CAROL: You read my letters

SHARON: That's different.

CAROL: Yeah?

SHARON: You left it on the table what was I meant to do
– 'sides I'm your friend – her she's a bloody sex witch –
you'll probably wake up to her lying in your bed one night
white robes chanting –

CAROL: Shut up will you.

SHARON goes to leave.

Now what.

SHARON: I'm going to get some Hob Nobs.

CAROL: I'll come with you.

SHARON: There's a hardware shop on the corner we could
have a look – see if they've got any locks.

Exit CAROL and SHARON.

Scene 2

Garden. KENNY and MICHAEL. KENNY fixing the van.

KENNY: Imagine infinity, the impossible enormity of it – if
you go far enough out into space you see everything,
right back from the beginning – see yourself born – go far
enough and nothing – Time collapses, the sheer volume
of nothingness, out of which – sometimes it gets so much –
you know – it's like my head's going to explode, I feel like
taking a drill to it.

MICHAEL: D'you want that sandwich?

KENNY: In each moment is enfolded all that has gone before – out of which enfolds all that will come.

MICHAEL: I'll have it if you don't.

KENNY: There is no future, only a continuous present.

MICHAEL takes sandwich.

MICHAEL: Thanks Ken. Here, does it run on petrol or d'you wind it up?

KENNY: Round the world son, round the bloody world son, you'll see. Pass me that spanner will you.

Goes under bonnet.

Shite – bloody foreign rubbish.

Scene 3

Front room. JOHN and NEIL.

JOHN: So what did you tell her? Come on.

NEIL: Fucking alternative comedians.

JOHN: Don't tell us then.

NEIL: I didn't say anything.

JOHN: You must've said something.

NEIL: I hate them.

JOHN: So you didn't say anything?

NEIL: I said... – ... I said –

JOHN: What?

NEIL: I said nothing.

JOHN: She told you to fuck off.

NEIL: What's it to you?

JOHN: You want to grow up you two or one of you's going to end up dead.

NEIL: They made Ben Elton look like Tommy Cooper.

JOHN: The beer's cheap.

NEIL: I don't like beer.

JOHN: What do you like?

NEIL: Tommy Cooper.

> *Enter MICHAEL.*

How's it going then Michael?

MICHAEL: Alright. You?

NEIL: Yeah, alright.

MICHAEL: You've been away.

NEIL: No.

MICHAEL: Oh. How was the pub?

JOHN: Yeah great.

NEIL: Right wing bastards, Tory sleepers.

MICHAEL: Who's that then?

NEIL: Your mob.

JOHN: He's getting you Guinness.

MICHAEL: Great.

JOHN: Got any skins?

> *Enter RAY with cans of beer.*

RAY: Here, have you seen –

NEIL: I hate them.

RAY: Have you seen –

JOHN: Watch it will you.

RAY: Over here, quick –

NEIL: Bloody pony tails.

> *RAY at window.*

RAY: On the corner, leopord skin mini skirt, thigh length leather boots, legs up to her neck –

NEIL: I hate them.

JOHN: What d'you get peanuts for?

RAY: She definitely give us the eye.

MICHAEL opens can.

MICHAEL: Cheers.

RAY: Bloody hell.

MICHAEL: So, you're moving out.

NEIL: Am I?

RAY: Aren't you?

NEIL: No.

MICHAEL: Oh.

RAY: She's just waiting.

JOHN: I can't eat these, they're dry roasted.

RAY: So?

JOHN: I wanted crisps.

RAY: I like nuts.

JOHN: I don't like dry roasted.

RAY: Don't eat them then.

MICHAEL: I'll have them.

NEIL: It's a right wing conspiracy to infiltrate the Labour Party and make it unelectable.

JOHN: Didn't they have any proper nuts?

RAY: Stop going on will you.

JOHN: I only like salted, take them back.

RAY: You've opened them.

NEIL: I hate them, the soft left.

RAY: What's the matter with him?

NEIL: Nothing.

JOHN: How's the Guinness?

MICHAEL: Yeah, alright.

JOHN: Knew I should've had Guinness.

RAY: Don't blame me.

JOHN: I'm not.

RAY looks out window.

RAY: She definitely give us the eye. Here, Sandra Finnigan was in the offie.

JOHN: So?

RAY: She read me palm.

JOHN: And?

RAY: And what?

JOHN: What did she say?

RAY: About what?

JOHN: Just forget it.

RAY: Forget what, what have I done?

NEIL: Nothing.

RAY: She said I was going to be a household name by the time I was forty.

JOHN: What for?

RAY: Dunno, didn't say – well I believe it.

NEIL: You would. Stupid cow.

MICHAEL: How d'you know she's stupid?

NEIL: Because she is.

RAY: Nice legs.

NEIL: (*To MICHAEL.*) Bloody Liberal.

JOHN: Got anything for a roach?

NEIL: Where are you going?

MICHAEL: I have to go.

JOHN: Stay and have another Guinness.

RAY gives JOHN a card.

MICHAEL: I can't.

RAY: Go on – we'll get some more cans in.

JOHN: You haven't got any money.

NEIL: I'll get them.

MICHAEL: No I'll get them.

Exit MICHAEL.

NEIL: Bloody Liberal.

JOHN: Where d'you get this?

RAY: Phone box on the corner.

JOHN: Looks like that actress.

RAY: Not a bad photo eh?

NEIL: What actress?

RAY: The one that looks like that bird you were chatting up in the pub the other night.

NEIL: Looks nothing like her.

RAY: Did you?

NEIL: Did I what?

RAY: Did you –

NEIL: No.

JOHN: (*Reading Card.*) 'What – U – see is what – U – get. Stunning blonde fantasy specialist. All services – including Greek'.

RAY: Greek, eh.

JOHN: Greek.

RAY: I'll ask her, next time I see that bird I'll ask her if you –

Enter CAROL and FRAN. NEIL hits RAY across head.

What d'you – Oh, hello Carol.

CAROL: Fran was just showing me her paintings.

RAY: I've got some etchings in me bedroom you can look at later if you like.

JOHN: Behave.

CAROL: They were great, I really liked them.

JOHN tears up card for roach.

RAY: Ah, what.

NEIL: Yeah, I really liked that one you did of Hell.

CAROL: Oh, which one was that?

FRAN: It got damaged.

NEIL: It was an accident.

FRAN: Would you like a drink Carol?

RAY: Here, if you won a million quid what would you do? I'd buy a bar in Spain, lie on the beach all day drinking shangrila's and retire.

FRAN: Sangrea.

JOHN: You've never worked.

RAY: Where's Sharon then Carol?

CAROL: She's gone home.

RAY: Give her a ring eh, get her round for a party.

CAROL: She's got work in the morning.

RAY: Could sleep here the night.

JOHN hits RAY on head.

What?

FRAN gives CAROL drink.

CAROL: Oh, thanks.

RAY: Use me mobile phone if you like.

JOHN: Waste of time you having that, nobody rings you.

RAY: Yeah they do.

JOHN: Yeah, your mam.

RAY: I like to be got hold of.

FRAN: If I won a million pounds I'd travel round the world
– leave this cold miserable damp little country and never
come back – the constant drone of small minds complaining about the weather.

NEIL: What would you do Carol?

CAROL: Me – Oh, I dunno – I'd buy me mam and dad a
house. I'd like to travel though – Sharon and me were
thinking of buying a van and driving round France this
summer.

RAY: Here what's Greek mean?

JOHN: Ring her and ask.

CAROL: This gin's very nice.

NEIL: I'd start a magazine.

RAY: You ring her.

JOHN: Shut up and skin up.

NEIL: The Radical Voice.

FRAN: More gin Carol.

RAY: Go on, ring her.

JOHN: You ring her.

RAY: Here, have you seen the workshop Carol? We're thinking of turning it into a recording studio.

FRAN: No we're not.

RAY: See what Carol thinks eh, then take a vote on it at the
next co-op meeting.

NEIL: Shut up Ray.

RAY: Well what good's it doing now, all bunged up with your
junk –

NEIL: Ray, I'm warning you.

CAROL: I've never lived anywhere as big as this before. It feels really lived in – you know.

RAY: Yeah.

CAROL: Really lived in.

FRAN: Sometimes I think of all the people that have lived here –

RAY: Oh no man, don't, don't get her started going on that.

CAROL: No, go on.

FRAN: All the people that have lived here and that will live here, over hundreds of years, the families, all those people –

Doorbell rings.

This house doesn't belong to anyone – we're just a part of that passing through.

NEIL: It belongs to the Council and they want to kick us out, pull it down.

JOHN: Yeah, it's a squat.

NEIL: It's not a squat, it's a co-op.

RAY: We go where we want, do what we want, say what we want – G'is a fag.

Doorbell rings.

JOHN: What is that?

RAY: The doorbell.

JOHN: We haven't got one.

RAY: Kenny fixed it up, found it in a skip.

NEIL: It'll be Michael.

JOHN: He's got a key.

FRAN: What's Michael got a key for?

JOHN: He does the garden.

FRAN: He doesn't live here.

Doorbell.

JOHN: Who the fuck is that?

RAY: How should I know.

JOHN: Go and look will you.

RAY: You look.

FRAN: Who gave Michael a key?

JOHN: I did, alright.

FRAN: No – I don't want Michael coming and going as he pleases, poking his nose in where it doesn't belong.

RAY: It's a copper.

NEIL: Ask him in for a smoke.

RAY: There's a copper I'm telling you.

Doorbell.

CAROL: Shouldn't we answer it? It might be important.

JOHN: Turn the light out. Fuck, there's a copper out there.

RAY: That's what I said isn't it.

JOHN: Answer the door then.

RAY: You answer it.

JOHN: Carol you answer it.

Exit FRAN.

CAROL: What shall I say?

JOHN: Nothing – just look at him and smile.

Door bell. Exit CAROL. RAY clears up all dope and exits. JOHN sits and reads. Enter FRAN with air freshener and sprays. Toilet flushing. Enter CAROL.

CAROL: Someone's left their car lights on out front and he wanted to know if it was anyone here.

Enter RAY.

JOHN: Skin up will you.

CAROL: See you in the morning – 'night.

Exit CAROL.

RAY: What, he didn't want anything then?

FRAN: No.

Exit FRAN.

JOHN: Skin up will you.

Sound of cistern fading.

RAY: No wait – don't get like that –

JOHN: You useless bastard.

RAY: John – no, don't – John.

Scene 4

Garden. KENNY by van reading letter.

KENNY: You will, you must, you must, you will, you will, if you do not –

Screws up letter.

Bloody fascists – that's right, that's what we need, everyone leading secure little lives in their own little boxes with their own little problems... I know this is my time to sit it out, to sit back and clean out my body wait till the time comes to act.

Throws letter away.

I don't need money to prove that I exist.

Scene 5

Front room. NEIL and FRAN.

NEIL: So he's back then – your feller.

FRAN: What feller?

NEIL: The feller you were shaggin' before christmas.

FRAN: And after.

NEIL: Yeah.

FRAN: D'you know if there's anything good on the telly?

NEIL throws open packet of condoms to FRAN.

NEIL: They were by your bed.

FRAN: What were you doing by my bed? Maybe we should get a video.

NEIL: Whose are they?

FRAN: I don't know.

NEIL: What were they doing by your bed? How did they get by your bed?

FRAN: I don't know. What were you doing in my bedroom? It's private.

NEIL: What's private?

FRAN: Christ, why is there never anything on the telly.

NEIL: So he's back then, the feller you were shagging before christmas and after.

FRAN: We don't live together anymore.

NEIL: We share a house.

FRAN: I haven't done anything wrong.

NEIL: I never said you had did I.

FRAN: You had no right.

NEIL: So whose are they?

FRAN: It's none of your business.

NEIL: They're yours.

FRAN: I don't like condoms. Huh.

NEIL: What?

FRAN: Nothing, a private thought.

NEIL: No – what. I just want to know that's all. It's him isn't it.

FRAN: Who?

NEIL: I don't know, you won't say.

FRAN: It's none of your bloody business.

NEIL: Just tell me.

FRAN: Bloody telly.

NEIL: I know who it is.

FRAN: You know so much you know everything, why bother asking me about it, you know so much you tell me. Did you look in the rubbish bin as well?

NEIL: I wasn't looking, right.

FRAN: I was even beginning to like you again.

NEIL: D'you want a drink?

FRAN: No – I don't want you in my bedroom again. I'm going out now, out to get a video – what do you want to do – stay here and go through my room again or come with me to make sure I don't shag anyone on the way?

NEIL: I'm going for a drink. You sure you don't want a drink.

FRAN: What do you want?

NEIL: I don't care anymore.

FRAN: So now you don't care.

NEIL: I don't know.

FRAN: You don't know what you want you've never known what you want.

NEIL: Do you care? I just want to know that's all, who is he?

FRAN: Little boys – little boys – they're all so, they're all so – at it all the time – you're so – you can't see... you just go on and on so there's no room for anyone else – I don't want you, I don't want you – it's got nothing to do with anyone else – it's you, you let me down, you let me down – it's not me you want –

NEIL: Who is it then?

FRAN: I don't know.

NEIL: No, who is it? Don't give me any of that shit – I know who I want.

FRAN: I can't just – it can't – you're so bloody wonderful so bloody bloody wonderful, you think you owe it to any woman so much as looks at you to stick your cock in them and light up their faces – who's she fucking is she with anyone else – it's all about you it's got nothing to do with me so you can keep your pathetic little male pride intact – you're so bloody marvellous, if I'm not with somebody else, why aren't I with you – there has to be somebody else, so you don't think, don't think about what you've done, what I feel, don't think about me – it's you, you, you, you, you, the world is you!

Enter CAROL with plate.

CAROL: Oh, I was just going to – You don't mind do you?

FRAN: No.

CAROL: It's just I'm late and –

FRAN: Sit down. Don't they feed you at work.

CAROL: Yeah, but I get sick of restaurant food.

FRAN: What's the name of it again?

CAROL: Le Mercury.

FRAN: You don't like the food?

CAROL: It's alright it's French. Cold isn't it?

FRAN: Yes.

CAROL: I've joined a women's group at the Irish Centre.

NEIL: Oh, I didn't know you were Irish.

CAROL: I'm not. D'you know it?

FRAN: No.

NEIL: What video are you going to get?

FRAN: I worked as a waitress once, the money was lousy.

CAROL: I make it up in tips.

FRAN: I'd like to do something useful.

CAROL: Wouldn't call it that.

NEIL: So you're not getting a video then.

FRAN: Something like a nun. When I was at school I used to go to bed in fear of waking up with a vocation, that God would call me in the night – now I'd almost welcome it.

Exit NEIL.

CAROL: Are you Catholic?

FRAN: No.

CAROL: Me neither – I believe in God though, well not so much as there's a God as some kind of universal spirit, an energy which we're all part of and come out of and go back in to, you know.

FRAN: I do, I wish I could do something really useful.

CAROL: Yeah.

FRAN: We should go out one night, you me and Karen.

CAROL: Sharon.

FRAN: I really liked her, she looked intuitive.

CAROL: What's the magazine?

FRAN: The New Statesman.

CAROL: Oh the New Statesman. You reading it?

FRAN: No, it's Neil's.

Enter NEIL with large notepad. Exit FRAN.

CAROL: D'you want some tea?

NEIL: I've already eaten thanks.

CAROL: A cup.

NEIL: Oh, no thanks.

CAROL: D'you always wear your collar up like that? Suits you.

NEIL opens notepad and writes.

What's that?

NEIL: Nothing – work.

CAROL: Is that your New Statement?

NEIL: Uh.

CAROL: Can I borrow it? Thanks – I like to have something to read in me break. No one tells you what to do do they – I could see that the first time I met you – the way you wear your collar up like that.

Scene 6

Kitchen. JOHN and RAY.

RAY: What are you doing with the light out?

JOHN: Want a fag?

RAY: Yeah alright.

JOHN: Those are mine, what are you doing with my sheets?

RAY: Washing.

JOHN: I didn't ask did I?

RAY: No.

JOHN gives RAY a cigarette.

Ta.

RAY lights cigarette.

Did you go up the bank today?

JOHN: No.

RAY: I thought you were going up the bank.

JOHN: It was closed.

RAY: So where have you been?

JOHN: Just about.

RAY: Fancy a drink? There's a couple of cans in the fridge. Come on let's have a drink.

JOHN: I've got coffee.

RAY: There's always the cashpoint next to the pub.

JOHN: I'm not going to the pub.

RAY: You what, we always go up the pub.

JOHN: Not tonight, alright.

RAY: Alright. I'll go if you like.

JOHN: I'll hit you if you don't stop it.

RAY: Alright. There's something going on, what's going on?

JOHN: Nothing's going on.

RAY: Why don't you want to go to the pub, we always go to the pub.

JOHN: I don't feel like it.

RAY: Why what's wrong?

JOHN: Nothing's wrong.

RAY: Come on. Look all I need's a fiver, just till tomorrow.

JOHN: No.

RAY: Why aren't you drinking?

JOHN: Who say's I'm not drinking?

RAY: You're not drinking, there's something up.

JOHN: What, what's up?

RAY: How should I know you won't tell me.

JOHN: There's nothing up, there's nothing going on, I haven't got a fiver and even if I did I wouldn't lend it to you.

RAY: Do your own bloody washing then, fucking fascist.

JOHN grabs RAY's arm twists it behind his back and pushes his face down on the table twisting his arm up.

JOHN: Come again.

RAY: Nothing.

JOHN: Say again.

RAY: Nothing.

JOHN: You owe me a fiver.

RAY: Leggo will you.

JOHN: You owe me a fiver.

RAY: Alright – alright.

    JOHN lets go of RAY.

    You could've broke me arm.

JOHN: Next time I will.

RAY: I was only joking.

JOHN: Yeah.

RAY: Yeah. It is it's broke.

JOHN: Good.

RAY: Haven't got any money – you've got money you're the co-op treasurer for fucksake, all you've got to do is write a bloody cheque, you're always doing it.

JOHN: I need Fran's signature.

RAY: Well get her to give you one.

JOHN: I've got the clap.

RAY: You what?

JOHN: You heard.

RAY: When?

JOHN: What d'you mean when, today when slaphead.

RAY: You've been down the clinic?

JOHN: No I went to give blood.

RAY: I've never had the clap.

JOHN: You don't shag – any woman so much as looks at you you run a mile, you don't like women, you never have, you're all mouth.

RAY: I shagged Sandra Finnigan.

JOHN: When?

RAY: Over the bank holiday.

JOHN: Slag.

RAY: You'll have to tell Lesley.

JOHN: What for?

RAY: She's your girlfriend.

JOHN: She's in Glasgow.

RAY: Maybe it was her that give it you.

JOHN: What you saying about my girlfriend.

RAY: Nothing.

JOHN: I'm gonna kill her.

RAY: Who?

JOHN: I will I'll kill her.

RAY: You'll have to tell her.

JOHN: I'm not telling Lesley, right.

RAY: Right. But what if you've –

JOHN: I haven't.

RAY: Yeah, but –

JOHN: I haven't.

RAY: You'll have to use a johnny then.

JOHN: How can you fuck someone with a johnny on.

RAY: But you might –

JOHN: I won't alright.

RAY: I didn't sleep with this girl once 'cos I thought I had the clap – she thought I was a gentleman.

JOHN: I'll kill her.

RAY: Who?

JOHN: You don't want to know.

RAY: Yeah I do.

JOHN: You don't.

RAY: I do.

JOHN: Sandra Finnigan.

RAY: You what?

JOHN: You heard.

RAY: When?

JOHN: Just before the bank holiday.

RAY: The slag, I'll kill her, I'll bloody kill her.

Scene 7

Front room. Mobile phone rings. RAY answers it.

RAY: Hello... you what?... who?... say again... Ray – Yeah, that's me – Ray – who? – you'll have to speak up it's the line... Oh mam – hello mam... you're in a phone box... I'll ring you back, give us your number... hang on. (*The phone cuts out.*) Useless Japanese crap.

Scene 8

CAROL's room. SHARON and CAROL with a tin of paint dustsheet and paintbrushes.

SHARON: So when am I going to meet this Neil.

CAROL: I don't know, when he's in.

SHARON: When's that?

CAROL: Sharon.

SHARON: Alright.

CAROL spreads dustsheet.

You don't want me to meet him. One look at me and he won't want to know about you.

CAROL: He's already got a girlfriend.

SHARON: So? She reminds me of one of those little mad dogs, you know, always snapping at your heels, scrunched up foreign mean piggy little eyes – they don't bark they squeel.

CAROL: This tin won't open.

SHARON: I told you you should've got white.

CAROL: What difference would that make?

SHARON: That'll just make the place look dirty.

CAROL: And since when have you been an expert?

SHARON: Since I did job experience as a beauty therapist.

CAROL: Have a brush.

SHARON: I love the smell of paint.

CAROL: Open a tin then.

SHARON: Martin came round this morning.

CAROL: Why didn't you say?

SHARON: I just did.

CAROL: I don't want to know.

SHARON: I don't know what you saw in him in the first place and as for that pony tail it's just bloody stupid, you can still see he's going bald.

CAROL: So what did he say?

CAROL begins to try and open the tin of paint.

SHARON: You'll need a screwdriver for that.

CAROL: So he didn't want anything?

SHARON: Thought you weren't interested.

CAROL: I'm not.

SHARON: He had a bunch of roses and a box of chocolates.

CAROL: Where are they then?

SHARON: I ate the chocolates and the roses are in water.

CAROL: They were for me.

SHARON: You're not talking to him.

CAROL: What sort of chocolates were they?

SHARON: Black Magic. Are all squats this bad.

CAROL: It's not a squat it's a co-op.

SHARON: Alright, no need to bite my head off.

CAROL has another go at opening the tin of paint.

It's raining.

CAROL: I know it's raining.

SHARON: You'd better empty those saucepans on the landing.

CAROL: I'll empty the saucepans when I empty them alright
– I don't need you telling me.

SHARON: What's the matter?

CAROL: Nothing's the matter.

SHARON: Come on.

CAROL: Nothing.

SHARON: All I said was –

CAROL: I know what you said – flippin' tin!

SHARON: We've got a new controller at work, drives a
Porsche, dead good looking, belongs to a health club at
the Holiday Inn, says I can get in on his membership – we

could go up one day, have a go on the sunbeds, lie around the pool drinking cocktails.

CAROL: You'll have to stop eating chocolates then won't you.

SHARON: Oh yeah?

CAROL: Yeah, you'd look disgusting in a bikini.

SHARON: I'll have to borrow one of yours then won't I.

Enter NEIL.

NEIL: I'm just off out to the shops, d'you want anything?

CAROL: Oh, no thanks. Neil Sharon, Sharon Neil.

NEIL: Nice to meet you. Looks good.

CAROL: I got Apple Blossom.

NEIL: Right.

SHARON: Could you get me a Flake.

She offers money.

NEIL: Oh, no, don't.

SHARON: Are you sure?

NEIL: Yeah. A Flake then.

SHARON: Carol was telling me you're a writer, what is it you write?

NEIL: Oh, you know – this and that – nothing serious.

CAROL: I expect you're in a rush.

SHARON: D'you write songs?

NEIL: No.

CAROL: Stop going on Sharon.

SHARON: I'm not, I'm just interested that's all, you don't mind do you – I've never met a writer before. So what do you write?

NEIL: I don't know – it's funny.

SHARON: Really.

NEIL: Funny with dark edges.

SHARON: I'll have to read some.

CAROL: You haven't got a screwdriver have you?

NEIL: No, not on me. A flake?

SHARON: Yeah.

Exit NEIL.

Doesn't know much about what he's doing does he – 'Funny with black edges', could be anything.

CAROL: God you're ignorant.

SHARON: Well you just stood there with your mouth open.

CAROL: And when was the last time you picked up a book let alone read one? And now you're an expert – it's always the same with you, anything you don't understand you have to knock it – you're just jealous.

SHARON: Why, why would I be jealous – what's to be jealous of !

Exit SHARON.

CAROL: Sharon.

Scene 9

Garden. MICHAEL stripped to waist sunbathing.

RAY: (*Offstage.*) It's true I'm telling you.

Laughter offstage.

FRAN: (*Offstage.*) Mind the step.

Laughter offstage. Enter SHARON with a bowl of strawberries.

SHARON: Where's the sun gone?

Looks at sky.

Ah, that's not fair. Pudding. It gets hot in there, even with the doors open. I like your tattoo. Beautiful creepers on the doo-dah.

MICAHEL: Vines.

SHARON: Oh.

Enter FRAN with plate of food.

FRAN: I told you to mind the step.

SHARON: Yeah.

FRAN offers plate to MICHAEL.

MICHAEL: No thanks, I've eaten.

FRAN: There's plenty left over.

MICHAEL: You look nice in that dress.

FRAN: It's summer, I feel summery.

Exit MICHAEL. Enter JOHN and RAY.

JOHN: He give us a tenner.

RAY: You what?

JOHN: You heard.

RAY: A tenner.

JOHN: Tight bastard.

FRAN: I'll get some sugar.

Exit FRAN. Enter CAROL.

KENNY: (*Offstage.*) If you're not part of the solution you're part of the problem!

SHARON: What was in that salad?

CAROL: Tomatoes, olive oil, vinegar, sugar, onion, coriander and capers – Fran made it.

SHARON: Tasted like weasel piss with iron filings.

RAY: You want to stick up for yourself, don't be such a shy boy, I'd have told him, said 'Where d'you think a tenner's gonna get me for the weekend?'

JOHN: Said that's all he had on him.

RAY: Oh yeah and what's he driving?

Enter FRAN.

JOHN: A Volvo estate.

FRAN: Sugar, Sharon?

SHARON: No thanks, just cream's fine.

FRAN: I love sugar and strawberries.

CAROL: She's on a diet.

SHARON: No I'm not.

FRAN: This heat, it's like the Mediterranean.

SHARON: Yeah.

CAROL heaps sugar into her bowl.

Why don't you just have done with it and stick them in the sugar bowl.

RAY: Bloody rich I hate the parasites – you don't want to go back – leave his house half painted.

JOHN: The best job I ever had was painting that chip shop on the King's Road.

RAY: Yeah.

CAROL: D'you like bowling?

FRAN: I've never been.

CAROL: We go every week, don't we Sharon?

SHARON: Yeah.

FRAN: A girls night out.

SHARON: Yeah.

CAROL: Is there a bowling alley round here?

FRAN: No, I'm afraid not.

SHARON: Shame.

FRAN: There's a wonderful women only gymnasium, with sauna, jacuzzi and Turkish bath – it's a sanctuary.

CAROL: We should all go bowling one night.

FRAN: I'd love to.

SHARON: Then we could all go for a Turkish bath.

FRAN: What a 'fab' idea.

CAROL: Yeah fab.

SHARON: Yeah fab.

Exit FRAN. NEIL and MICHAEL in the kitchen.

MICHAEL: Nigel.

NEIL: Nigel Bewdley.

MICHAEL: He's dead now, got killed hang gliding.

NEIL: When they found Janice Ferguson I wanted to go round and punch her in the face for killing herself.

MICHAEL: He had two kids.

NEIL: Yeah.

MICHAEL: Little girl little boy. Have you ever thought about –

NEIL: No never.

KENNY, CAROL, JOHN, RAY and SHARON in garden. SHARON smoking a joint.

JOHN: She went to Malvern to do a course on connecting with the infinite self and never came back.

RAY: Finish it if you like.

SHARON: No thanks.

Hands RAY joint.

JOHN: Connected with an aromatherapist from South Wales called Justin.

RAY: Yeah, he put her in touch with herself.

Exit SHARON.

Something she ate.

CAROL: Oh no, the food was delicious.

KENNY: You want to stop that, it's poison.

RAY: Yeah.

Exit RAY.

CAROL: This heat, it's like the Mediterranean.

JOHN: Cornwall's the place to be when it gets like this.

KENNY: You want to expand your horizons – Bali, Asia, the Far East.

JOHN: Yeah, Morocco.

CAROL: What's that jug for by the pond? Looks like an alter.

JOHN: Kenny's mate.

KENNY: A funeral urn.

CAROL: What happened?

KENNY: He died, alright.

Exit KENNY.

JOHN: Don't mind him. We buried the ashes under a willow tree.

CAROL: What happened to the tree?

JOHN: It got blown away.

RAY and SHARON.

RAY: You alright?

SHARON: Yeah.

RAY: You should eat something – have a bit of chicken.

SHARON: No thanks, I'm a vegetarian.

RAY: Go on, do you good.

SHARON: Oh alright, I'll have a sausage roll.

RAY: I'll give you a massage if you like.

SHARON: No thanks.

Exit RAY. NEIL and FRAN in the kitchen.

NEIL: I'm going to Scotland.

FRAN: Live where you want.

NEIL: I live here.

FRAN: Open this will you.

Gives him a bottle of wine.

NEIL: It's a wedding.

FRAN: The garden looks so pretty in this light – Michael's such a good gardener, I should recommend him to mummy's friends – they've all got such big gardens.

NEIL: You could paint murals for them.

Enter RAY.

RAY: We got any water left?

NEIL: No.

RAY: I'll take it from tap.

FRAN: It's polluted.

RAY: I only want a cup.

NEIL: Give her a cup while you're at it will you.

RAY: I'll go and buy a bottle.

Exit RAY. NEIL gives FRAN bottle opened.

FRAN: Piss off to Scotland Neil.

NEIL: Just grow up will you.

Exit FRAN and NEIL. CAROL, SHARON, JOHN and RAY in garden.

SHARON: He's a pervert.

CAROL: He only offered to give you a massage.

SHARON: Your mind's twisted, they've twisted your mind.

CAROL: My mind's twisted.

SHARON: You'll be into free love next.

JOHN: It's a full moon.

RAY howls like a wolf.

SHARON: Oh, I shouldn't've had that cigarette.

CAROL: What cigarette?

SHARON: The one that John give me – I didn't want to be rude, he rolled it himself.

Enter KENNY and NEIL.

KENNY: It's inner revelation leads to revolution – all societies are a form of tyranny.

RAY: Eh up, Kenny's off again.

NEIL: It's about class, it's about money and anybody that thinks different needs a hole in their head.

Exit NEIL.

RAY: Here Ken, how's the van going, what you doing with it now?

KENNY: That's not the question – what's the van doing with me.

JOHN: This is God Ken, he's got a message for you – You will do all the cleaning in the house – You will cook all John's meals for two weeks and make sure there's always toilet paper in the bog.

RAY: You will steal money and give it to Ray.

CAROL goes to leave.

SHARON: Carol.

CAROL: What.

JOHN: Here you go Ken, have a glass of wine.

Exit CAROL.

SHARON: D'you really think that about your van.

KENNY: Why not?

SHARON: You think it's got a life of it's own?

KENNY: Don't be bloody stupid, it's a van.

RAY: Look a space ship.

KENNY: There'll be people living on Mars in two hundred years time.

IRISH MAN: (*Offstage.*) All our neighbours are fucking wankers!

SHARON: One of those boys is going to fall off that roof if they don't watch it.

Music. Exit KENNY and SHARON. NEIL and CAROL in front room.

CAROL: What you doing?

NEIL: Nothing.

CAROL: What's the music?

NEIL: Jazz. D'you like jazz?

CAROL: No.

NEIL: Me neither.

CAROL: Everyone's still out in the garden. Not the sort of music you can dance to.

NEIL: No.

NEIL turns off music.

CAROL: It's turned cold – I came in for a coat.

NEIL takes off jacket and gives it to her.

Thanks. Come on.

Exit CAROL and NEIL. JOHN, RAY and FRAN in the garden.

JOHN: Here, Fran, are you going away this summer?

FRAN: Maybe – I've been invited to Lanzarote for September.

RAY: I'll come with you if you like – carry the bags.

JOHN: No, I was just thinking if you were, it might be as well to leave a couple of co-op cheques signed, in case of an emergency.

Enter SHARON.

SHARON: Have you seen Carol?

FRAN: No.

Exit FRAN.

RAY: Stay and have a drink with us.

SHARON: I think I'll go and lie down for a while.

Exit SHARON. NEIL and CAROL lying in garden.

CAROL: I could look at them forever.

NEIL: It takes a hundred thousand million stars to make up a galaxy – huge islands turning like gigantic wheels, separated by vast stretches of space.

CAROL: Really?

NEIL: Yeah – I read it on the back of a matchbox.

CAROL: You're daft you.

NEIL: Yeah.

CAROL: Yeah.

CAROL sits up.

NEIL: Make you feel small don't they.

CAROL: What?

NEIL: Nothing.

CAROL: Go on.

NEIL: Everything that happens... it happens through us – we're all connected... we have the choice and we choose to do nothing.

CAROL: About what?

NEIL: You look nice.

CAROL: Give over.

NEIL: No I'm serious.

CAROL: I'd better go and find Sharon – she'll be wondering what's happened.

Exit CAROL and NEIL. RAY and JOHN in garden. JOHN laughing.

RAY: What? What's the joke? What you laughing at?

JOHN: Sex.

RAY: What?

JOHN: Sex is funny.

Scene 10

Kitchen. FRAN and MICHAEL.

MICHAEL: I thought you didn't smoke.

FRAN: I don't.

  She lights cigarette.

MICHAEL: So, how are you?

FRAN: Fine.

MICHAEL: I just want a room that's all.

FRAN: There aren't any.

MICHAEL: You still seeing that spiritual Guru of yours –
   shagging your way to Nirvana on Tuesdays.

  Laughing offstage.

CAROL: No, don't.

NEIL: I never touched you.

CAROL: You'll wake everyone.

  Enter CAROL and NEIL.

FRAN: How was the play?

CAROL: Yeah, great – is that the time?

MICHAEL: I'm going then.

NEIL: What, no coffee?

MICHAEL: Not tonight, no.

  Exit MICHAEL.

FRAN: So, you had a good time?

CAROL: Brilliant.

NEIL: How was Michael?

CAROL: The sets were amazing – wardrobes stretching up to the ceiling and all the doors at funny angles.

FRAN: Sounds like a pantomime.

NEIL: Why don't you go and see it first.

FRAN: What's the matter with you?

NEIL: Nothing – I just don't like the way you have to knock everything.

FRAN: It's not my fault I haven't got your taste.

NEIL: So how was Michael?

FRAN: See you in the morning – don't forget to turn the light out.

Exit FRAN.

CAROL: I'd better get off to bed as well – I have to, I'm on at lunchtime. Thanks, I did enjoy it, really.

NEIL: What – oh, no point getting excited it's only a play.

CAROL: I like the way you don't care – you just say what you think.

NEIL kisses her. She pushes him away.

ACT TWO

Scene 1

Front room. RAY, JOHN, FRAN, CAROL and KENNY.

RAY: There's not enough glasses.

    RAY hands CAROL joint.

CAROL: No thanks.

RAY: Go on.

CAROL: I don't.

    Gives it to JOHN.

RAY: There's not enough glasses.

JOHN: Get some mugs then.

RAY: I'm not using a mug.

CAROL: Don't worry about me.

RAY: I tell you, I'm not using a mug.

JOHN: I'll have a bloody mug then.

RAY: Red or white?

CAROL: I'm not drinking thanks.

JOHN: Have a drink.

FRAN: I'm going if you two get drunk.

JOHN: Who's drunk?

RAY: Red or white?

FRAN: We vetoed all drugs from meetings.

RAY: Yeah, that's right, I remember that.

JOHN: What drugs?

FRAN: What do you call that?

JOHN: Wine.

RAY: Red or white?

FRAN: Red.

JOHN: You don't want red, it goes right to your head.

FRAN: I like red.

JOHN: Alright.

CAROL: I've never been to a co-op meeting before.

RAY offers her the joint.

RAY: Have some of this. You can take the minutes if you like.

JOHN: You take the minutes.

RAY: I took them last time.

CAROL: I don't mind taking the minutes.

FRAN: Take the minutes Ray.

RAY: Ah, that's not fair – you're always picking on me – why's it always me does them when was the last time you did them?

JOHN: I'm the treasurer.

RAY: Yeah.

JOHN pulls out a fiver.

JOHN: So go and get another bottle.

RAY: Right.

RAY gets up to go.

FRAN: Just sit down will you.

RAY: We haven't started yet.

FRAN stands. RAY sits. FRAN sits.

KENNY: Stop fucking about will you.

RAY: Why don't we just tape it.

Enter NEIL.

FRAN: Where have you been?

NEIL: What's it to you?

FRAN: You're late.

RAY: Red or white?

NEIL: Red please.

FRAN: You're late.

NEIL: No I'm not.

FRAN: You're late.

JOHN: Grow up the pair of you.

RAY: We're definitely going to need more red.

FRAN: You owe us an apology.

NEIL: I don't owe you anything.

JOHN: Right, so are we quorate or what?

RAY: There's Michael to come.

JOHN: He's not a co-op member.

RAY: He does the garden.

FRAN: What's Michael coming for?

RAY: He does the garden.

FRAN: Oh no, he's not moving in, I'm not having him live here.

NEIL: Who said he wants to move in.

RAY: Anyroad what's wrong with him.

FRAN: So why else is he doing the garden.

RAY: Bloody rich I hate the parasites. (*To FRAN.*) You know what I could do to you I could rip your belly open with my teeth and pull out your guts with my bare hands.

NEIL: Fuck off will you.

JOHN: Finished?

RAY: No.

FRAN: We'll start with the minutes.

RAY: Don't look at me.

JOHN: You took them.

RAY: So.

NEIL: Where are they?

Enter MICHAEL.

MICHAEL: Sorry I'm late.

FRAN: So there aren't any?

RAY: I just don't know where I put them, that's all.

NEIL: Ray, do you like living here – do you want it to be anymore than Short Life – then sit up, open your eyes, take the notes and don't skin up another joint.

JOHN: Fascist. They're never gonna kick us out, they haven't got the money to Re-hab, they're bankrupt.

NEIL: So maybe they'll knock the place down.

RAY: And build what?

NEIL: A car park.

FRAN gets up to leave.

Where are you going?

JOHN: Michael hasn't given his report on the garden yet.

MICHAEL: Oh, don't worry about me.

FRAN: I'm not.

NEIL: We've got an agenda to get through.

FRAN: What agenda?

NEIL hands round agenda.

NEIL: (*To FRAN.*) Satisfied?

RAY: (*To CAROL.*) Got a fag?

CAROL: I don't smoke.

JOHN: Here.

JOHN throws RAY a cigarette.

RAY: Ta. Sorry about that.

FRAN sits.

JOHN: Hang on, what's this – item number one treasurer's report – no one told me I had to give a report, fuck that.

RAY: You want me to write that down? Alright, only a joke.

NEIL: (*To JOHN.*) Well?

JOHN: We've got four thousand pounds in the bank.

RAY: Bloody hell.

FRAN: And that's it?

JOHN: Yeah.

RAY: Hold on – what have we got four thousand pounds in the bank for?

NEIL: Maintenance and repairs – the fighting fund.

CAROL puts her hand up.

RAY: Who are we fighting?

FRAN: Carol.

CAROL: Couldn't we spend some of that money on fixing the roof?

NEIL: Great idea.

FRAN: Yeah, great Carol – you can set up a working party to investigate the feasibility and costing of repairing the roof.

JOHN: It doesn't need repairing, it needs replacing – the timbers are rotten – the slates are hanging off like loose teeth.

CAROL: What's a working party?

RAY: Hang about – 'A working party into – ' then what?

FRAN: Investigating the feasibility and costing of repairing the roof.

CAROL: Sorry, but what's a working party?

NEIL: I'll go over it with you later.

FRAN: Rent arrears.

JOHN: Yeah they're fine – we're all behind.

FRAN: Nobody's got anything to say?

RAY puts his hand up.

Ray.

RAY: Yeah – well – I was wondering, why pay rent at all – I mean the Council don't charge us anything, we don't pay Rates anymore, so why charge ourselves –

NEIL: Give over Ray.

RAY: Well at least a rent cut then – taking into account the Council Tax.

JOHN: You don't pay the bloody Council Tax.

RAY: I'm serious.

NEIL: You're serious?

RAY: Yeah.

NEIL: Alright – well I propose we all join the Labour Party.

JOHN: Oh no, not again.

NEIL: He's serious, I'm serious.

JOHN: I'm not joining any Party.

RAY: What about a rent cut?

FRAN: No one should be forced to join any political organisation they don't want to.

NEIL: Bloody Liberals.

RAY: They're all a load of bollocks if you ask me.

NEIL: So what does it matter then?

RAY: I don't vote.

NEIL: I just want to go on living here Ray – what about you?

FRAN: Do you?

NEIL: Yes.

JOHN: Opportunist bastard.

NEIL: Where were you when the miners were on strike.

KENNY: Why don't you all just fuck off to Vietnam.

RAY: So, what about a rent cut then?

FRAN: We'll think about it, alright.

NEIL: You can't sign your names without having to think about it – No, I want a motion – I propose we all join the Labour Party.

FRAN: So, the motion is we all join the Labour Party?

RAY: Say again.

NEIL: Fuck off.

FRAN: Who'll second it?

CAROL: I'll second it.

RAY: You don't have to.

CAROL: I want to.

FRAN: Those in favour?

> *NEIL and CAROL.*

Those against?

> *The rest.*

NEIL: This co-op's still got a squatter hippie mentality – doped up, spaced out, two freaks and a dog – you're all stuck still dropping acid at a House Party, somewhere in the seventies.

FRAN: Shut up Neil.

NEIL: You've got that?

RAY: Yeah.

NEIL: You've written that down?

RAY: Yeah.

FRAN: Satisfied?

NEIL: No.

FRAN: Michael.

MICHAEL: What.

FRAN: You're still with us?

MICHAEL: Yeah, oh yeah – the garden.

JOHN: Well I think it looks great.

RAY: Yeah, the pond looks great.

MICHAEL: It's just the grass really – round the pond – it needs returfing.

JOHN: How much will it cost?

MICHAEL: I don't know yet – I've got to meet this bloke in the pub about it.

JOHN: Well I vote we give Michael the go ahead.

RAY: I'll second that.

FRAN: All those for?

All but NEIL.

Those against?

NEIL.

You're not voting together this time. Any other business.

JOHN: Yeah – the caravan.

FRAN: No – it's not fit to live in.

RAY: Hang on –

NEIL: There's a waiting list.

JOHN: How long did you wait on it?

FRAN: It's not habitable.

RAY: But –

JOHN: Forget it.

RAY: Bloody fascists.

KENNY: Bloody fascists, there are too many fascists in this world brother – undercover slippery bloody fascists, they're all working for the government – and they're not getting paid for it – we've got neighbourhood watch, we've got – all ready to grass you up for nothing.

JOHN: Right then –

FRAN: The meeting isn't over. I'd like to propose that from now on all co-op members leave the toilet seat down when they're finished. I don't see why it should always be left up when you're finished. It presumes the next person going is male.

NEIL: Isn't it sexist either way?

RAY: Maybe we should take it off altogether.

FRAN: It says women exist as second class citizens.

RAY: Alright, so we'll leave it down and piss all over the seat – can I go now. Well?

FRAN throws glass of wine in RAY's face.

Scene 2

Garden. SHARON and MICHAEL.

SHARON: Nice garden. Pity about the rain – that why you stopped digging is it? Nice to have somewhere to sit out – where I live we just look out on a brick wall. Don't say much, do you? I don't talk much sometimes – I just like to sit in front of the telly with a gin and tonic. Good with that fork aren't you. What?

MICHAEL: Nothing.

FRAN and NEIL in front room.

NEIL: You alright?

FRAN: Fucking work, fucking house, fucking life – it's because I'm small, because I look younger than I am, because I'm a woman.

NEIL: It's alright.

Puts his arms around her.

You'll be alright.

Rocks her gently. SHARON and MICHAEL in the garden.

SHARON: Do you like gardening?

MICHAEL: Not much.

SHARON: I've never done any. I like gardens though. What do you do?

MICHAEL: I'm a gardener.

SHARON: You don't live here then?

MICHAEL: No.

SHARON: You don't live in a co-operative.

MICHAEL: No.

SHARON: So how do you know this lot?

MICHAEL: I used to live in a squat with Neil.

SHARON: I used to have a bank account with The Co-op.

MICAHEL: What?

SHARON: I'm a friend of Carol's. D'you know her?

MICHAEL: No.

SHARON: I'm waiting for her.

MICHAEL: I'd best be going then.

CAROL: You don't have to go.

MICHAEL: I have to get back.

SHARON: Might see you around.

MICHAEL: Yeah.

SHARON: I'm Sharon.

MICHAEL: Michael. Would you like to go for a drink.

SHARON: I'm waiting for Carol.

MICHAEL: Tonight.

SHARON: I would if I could but I can't – I've got something on.

MICHAEL: Oh, I see.

SHARON: Maybe another night.

MICHAEL: Yeah.

SHARON: What's your number?

MICHAEL: I haven't got a phone.

Exit MICHAEL.

Scene 3

Kitchen. JOHN listening to music. Enter RAY.

JOHN: Anyone rings I'm out.

RAY: You're always out.

RAY turns off music.

JOHN: He's got someone up there.

JOHN turns on music.

RAY: No he hasn't.

RAY turns off music.

JOHN: He's got someone up there I'm telling you.

RAY: Well I can't hear anything.

JOHN: Listen.

Silence.

RAY: See.

JOHN: They've been at it all afternoon.

RAY: You should've gone out.

JOHN: I didn't feel like it.

RAY: So, who's he got up there?

JOHN: How should I know, he didn't stop to say – put his head round the door and say 'Hello John, this is Seretta I'm just taking her upstairs to shag the arse off her'.

RAY: Saw Sandra Finnigan down the pub.

JOHN: What did she say?

RAY: About what?

Phone rings.

JOHN: I'm out.

RAY: You're never in.

JOHN: I like being out. What's to eat?

RAY: Didn't you do any shopping?

JOHN: Let it ring. What's in the fridge?

RAY: Nothing.

JOHN: How about a glass of wine.

RAY: I'll have to go out.

JOHN: Forget it.

RAY: Well I wouldn't mind a glass.

JOHN: You've only just got back from the pub.

RAY: I need a drink.

JOHN: You drink too much.

Phone stops.

RAY: Phone's stopped.

JOHN: God you're hopeless – like that time you scored a bottle of asprin.

RAY: He said they were E's.

JOHN: Thirty quid for a couple of asprin – bloody hopeless.

They've taken me dad into hospital.

RAY: I'll go and get a bottle of wine.

JOHN: What was his name.

RAY: He'll be alright.

JOHN: The feller that sold you the asprin.

RAY: Dave – I don't know, tall bloke, glasses, you know you nicked his motorbike.

JOHN: It was my thirty quid that paid for the asprin.

RAY: Not your money, the house's money.

RAY smiles.

JOHN: No – no – no!

RAY: Yeah, we should – buy a load of drugs with it and retire to Brazil.

JOHN: (*Together.*) Ronnie Biggs!

RAY: (*Together.*) Ronnie Biggs!

JOHN: It's serious this time.

RAY: He'll be alright.

JOHN: Yeah.

RAY: Have you got her to sign a cheque yet?

JOHN: No.

KENNY: (*Offstage.*) Louder... Louder... Louder... Yeah – now we're getting somewhere.

JOHN: Told you he had someone up there.

Scene 4

Front room. NEIL and FRAN. NEIL half dressed in front of a long mirror.

NEIL: I look like shit.

FRAN: You look great.

NEIL: No I don't.

FRAN: You look alright.

NEIL: Like shit.

FRAN: You look great.

NEIL: You're just saying that. What about the shirt?

FRAN: Yeah, it's okay. It's smart.

NEIL: You don't think it should be black, with a white tie?

FRAN: No – you'd look like a gangster. You look great.

NEIL: You really think so?

FRAN: Dressed to kill.

NEIL: I don't want to look dressed to kill.

FRAN: Why not, it's a wedding, you might meet someone nice.

NEIL: Stop it will you.

FRAN: What?

NEIL: Look I'm only going because they're old friends, because –

FRAN: Because –

NEIL: Because they're old friends.

FRAN: It doesn't bother me, sleep with who you like.

NEIL: Bloody tie.

FRAN: Maybe you're right, maybe a black shirt and a white tie would look better. What about one of your Hawaiian shirts?

NEIL: You just want me to look ridiculous.

FRAN: You are ridiculous. Ring them up and ask if Nellie's going.

NEIL: Lottie.

FRAN: Lottie.

NEIL puts trousers on.

NEIL: What about the present, d'you think they'll like their present? They won't like it, I know they won't. I've never been any good at buying presents.

FRAN: I liked that scarf you bought me.

NEIL: What scarf, I never bought you any scarf – who bought you a scarf?

FRAN: They'll like it.

NEIL: Anyway, you're easy to buy presents for, you like anything.

FRAN: Yeah, I've got no taste.

NEIL: I can't go. I look like shit.

FRAN: You look great and the yucca plant's unbelieveable.

NEIL: Stop taking the piss. You're always taking the piss.

FRAN: Come here. Come here will you – it's your hair.

NEIL: What's wrong with it?

FRAN: Come here.

She kisses him. NEIL breaks away.

NEIL: What about the shoes – Christ I've only got black and they should be brown with white trousers – I've only got black, I haven't got brown.

FRAN: Then black will have to do.

NEIL: They should be brown.

FRAN: They're alright.

NEIL: What's the matter?

FRAN: Nothing.

NEIL: I was worried about my shoes.

FRAN: They're fine, you're fine, there's no need to worry.

Enter JOHN.

JOHN: Oh, sorry I just –

FRAN: What?

JOHN: No, it can wait.

FRAN: What?

JOHN: Just these cheques – they can wait.

FRAN: No.

NEIL lights cigarette. FRAN signs cheques.

Just the two.

JOHN: Make it three if you like – just to be safe. You're off to Scotland then?

NEIL: Yeah.

JOHN: I like porridge. Ta.

JOHN takes cheque book and exits.

FRAN: You should stop smoking.

NEIL: I can't.

FRAN: Try herbal cigarettes then.

NEIL: Stop taking the piss.

FRAN: I'm not.

NEIL: I'm going up in the car with Lottie. It'll save money.

FRAN: I'll give you money.

NEIL: I don't want your money.

FRAN: Why not?

NEIL: I'm tired alright.

FRAN: It's always the same – 'I'm tired', 'I haven't got any money' – anything to avoid saying 'I want to do this', 'I choose to do this'.

NEIL: Alright, so I want to go in the car with her.

FRAN: So why didn't you say?

NEIL: Because you always think something's going on – that I'm going to screw her in-between gear shifts.

FRAN: You can always stop the car.

NEIL: You see, there you go, accusing me of something I haven't done.

FRAN: I really don't care, do what you want.

NEIL: You're such a bloody saint aren't you – why, why d'you do this to me?

FRAN: I'm not doing anything.

Scene 5

Kitchen. Music. RAY cutting up an old rag. A plate smashes offstage. Music stops. Enter KENNY.

KENNY: Jesus Christ, bloody 'Rhythms of The World' – who the fuck listens to World Music!

Exit KENNY. Enter JOHN.

JOHN: What are you doing?

RAY: Cutting up this old rag.

JOHN: That's not an old rag, that's my sweatshirt.

RAY: Oh.

JOHN: Look at it – I was gonna iron that.

RAY: I'll buy you another.

JOHN: Yeah.

RAY: So?

JOHN: Put the kettle on.

RAY: Where is it?

JOHN: Put the kettle on.

RAY: You didn't get it.

JOHN takes out a bundle of notes. RAY takes the money.

I'm not gonna wash this hand for a week.

JOHN: Five hundred.

RAY: Five hundred – I love you – I love you man – I love you –

RAY kisses JOHN. Enter KENNY.

KENNY: Been up the bank eh?

They stop kissing.

JOHN: It's a win Ken, I had a win on the horses.

RAY: Yeah – Madam Frascati.

KENNY: How much d'you win?

RAY: (*Together.*) Five hundred pounds.

JOHN: (*Together.*) Two hundred and fifty –

KENNY takes out the co-op cheque book and puts it on table.

KENNY: I found this in the hall. That's one hundred and sixty seven point three three recurring each.

JOHN: Hang about Ken.

KENNY: I could pick up a reasonable clutch for that.

RAY: You don't need money Ken, you don't believe in it.

KENNY: A clutch that's all I need. I need a clutch and God has provided.

Scene 6

Front room. CAROL and SHARON.

SHARON: What are you doing in that?

CAROL: It's a kimono.

SHARON: I know what it is – you didn't buy it did you?

CAROL: Fran gave it me.

SHARON: You're not sick are you?

CAROL: No.

SHARON: Well you'd better get dressed or we'll be late.

CAROL: Leave it alone.

SHARON: It's attacking me.

CAROL: Just leave it.

SHARON: Bloody bee.

CAROL: It won't hurt you.

SHARON: Thats easy for you to say, it's not you it's trying to sting.

SHARON swats at bee.

CAROL: Don't.

SHARON: I hate bees.

CAROL: What d'you want to kill it for?

SHARON: It's attacking me.

CAROL: Its bad karma.

SHARON: I don't care what it is, I don't like getting stung.

CAROL: Just sit still and it'll go away. Sit still will you. See.

SHARON swats at the table.

SHARON: Got the little bugger.

CAROL: What did you do that for?

SHARON: I told you, I hate bees.

CAROL: Its bad karma, it'll come back on you.

SHARON: Don't talk soft.

CAROL: You don't care do you.

SHARON: No.

CAROL: You don't care about anything.

SHARON: You're on drugs aren't you – look at me, look me in the eyes, come on – you are, you're on something, you've got pupils the size of golfballs, what are you on.

CAROL: Nothing.

SHARON: What have you been taking?

CAROL: Let go will you. I'm not on anything right.

SHARON: And I suppose all this karma stuff came with the kimono did it? Come on get dressed.

CAROL: In a minute.

SHARON: It starts at seven thirty

CAROL: What?

SHARON: You are, you're on something.

CAROL: I don't like being rushed.

SHARON: What d'you mean rushed – its six o'clock and you've only just got out of bed. Alright, we'll wait, but don't blame me if we're late.

Are you getting dressed or what?

CAROL: No.

SHARON: You can't go out like that.

CAROL: I don't feel like going out.

SHARON: We always go out on a Wednesday.

CAROL: Not written in stone is it?

SHARON: So you're not coming out then?

CAROL: No.

SHARON: Why not?

CAROL: I've said.

SHARON: You don't feel like it.

CAROL: Yeah.

SHARON: Well I don't feel like going out on me own, I'll stop in with you.

CAROL: Just leave me alone will you.

SHARON: Right. Well I hope he's worth it.

CAROL: Who?

SHARON: You know who I mean.

CAROL: I'm staying in because I want to. Look – what about Friday?

SHARON: Maybe – I don't know yet, I might have something on, or I might want to stay in and be left alone with the telly.

Exit SHARON.

Scene 7

Kitchen. FRAN chanting on table.

FRAN: I – I – I – I – I – I – I – I – I – I – I – I – I – I – I – I –
    I – I – I – I – I will not be – of course I have feelings... I will
    feel... I have feelings... I am me... I am me... I – I – I – ... I will
    not be part of the deceit... I will not be part of the pretence... I
    will not be part of the collusion...

Enter JOHN.

JOHN: Sorry, I didn't realize –

FRAN: No, don't go. Neil rang.

JOHN: How's the wedding?

FRAN: I don't know – he rang to say he was in a phone box, that
    he wasn't going to sleep with her, that they've got separate
    rooms in separate hotels – then his money ran out.

JOHN: He'll ring back.

FRAN: Like hell.

JOHN: Ring his hotel.

FRAN: He didn't leave a number.

JOHN: He'll ring back.

FRAN: Yeah.

JOHN: He probably just forgot.

FRAN: Yeah, like he's not sleeping with her – until this even-
    ing, when he's blind drunk and then it won't be his fault,
    it'll just happen and then he'll feel bad and he'll make me
    suffer, as if it was my fault he feels bad and deep down he
    knows I feel fucking awful, but somehow it's all my fault
    – that I'm stopping him from being who he is, when he
    doesn't even know who the fuck he is, if it wasn't for the
    shaving mirror he wouldn't have a clue, he wouldn't know
    who the fuck he was.

JOHN: I'll have a word with him if you like – no I didn't mean – what? No, go on what's funny.

If there's anything you need – just say.

FRAN: A Turkish bath.

JOHN: Oh yeah – where d'you go for that, Turkey? I've never had a Turkish bath, what's it like?

FRAN: Wonderful – you can stay in it for hours, soak in the steam.

JOHN: You don't sweat then? I sweat like a pig.

FRAN: They scrape off the dirt.

JOHN: How much does that cost?

FRAN: Eight pounds.

JOHN: Eight pounds for a bath?

FRAN: Yes, but it's worth it.

JOHN: Bar of soap only costs fifty pence.

FRAN laughs.

You should do that more often, it suits you.

Scene 8

Kitchen. RAY, JOHN and KENNY.

RAY: If someone asked you to whip them, what would you say?

JOHN: Why?

RAY: No reason – I was just wondering.

JOHN: What for?

RAY: Forget it.

JOHN: Who's asking?

RAY: No one.

JOHN: So why ask:

RAY: Just forget it.

JOHN: Have a banana.

> *JOHN throws RAY a banana. RAY holds it to his ear.*

RAY: There's no one there – get it eh – there's no one there. But what would you say?

JOHN: Nothing – I'd beat the shit out of you.

RAY: Not me, someone else.

JOHN: Like who?

RAY: I dunno – a woman.

JOHN: I wouldn't say anything.

RAY: No, you wouldn't would you.

JOHN: Who you – me you, or you you?

RAY: You you. I couldn't do it.

JOHN: You're too romantic, that's your trouble. How's the van Ken?

RAY: G'is the water.

JOHN: He's not in.

RAY: Lights are on.

JOHN: You still with us Kenny.

KENNY: Yeah, now fuck off.

JOHN: (*As KENNY.*) Yeah, now fuck off.

RAY: (*As KENNY.*) Yeah, now fuck off.

KENNY: Fuck off.

RAY: G'is the water.

JOHN: You've got beer.

RAY: I want water.

JOHN: Get your own.

RAY: Its mine. It is – cost me fifty-nine pence that.

JOHN: No it didn't – cost me eighty-nine round the Paki's.

RAY: It cost me fifty-nine.

JOHN: Eighty-nine.

RAY: Fifty-nine.

JOHN: Eighty-nine.

RAY: Fifty-nine.

JOHN: Eighty-nine.

RAY: Fifty-nine.

JOHN: Eighty-nine.

> *JOHN throws water to RAY.*

> What you doing Ken?

> *RAY drinks water.*

> I spat in that. Good is it Ken?

RAY: I bet you did n' all.

> *JOHN does sit ups.*

> What you doin'?

JOHN: Getting fit.

RAY: Fit for what?

JOHN: For Kenny's van for what – he's taking us round the world in it, aren't you Ken?

RAY: He could take us to Brighton – got any wheels for it yet Ken – you're not fit.

JOHN: I'm fit, right.

RAY: Yeah.

JOHN: I'm fit – you, you're gonna explode by the time you're thirty, your whole body's going to flab – you want to take a look in the mirror, the rings under your eyes – black, that's your liver that is, it's packing up on you – you do too much of this that's your trouble.

RAY: I take vitamins.

JOHN: And the rest.

RAY: When was the last time you didn't skin up for breakfast?

JOHN: Here, Kenny – quick, look – there's an army of Martians walking down the street, all green heads and testicles.

RAY: Tentacles.

JOHN: Hang on, one of them's red, what's that mean?

RAY: Stop taking the piss.

JOHN: What's the matter with you?

RAY: Nothing. Here, d'you think there are Kenny? Kenny!

KENNY: What?

RAY: D'you think there are.

KENNY: What, are what?

RAY: Aliens. No, serious.

KENNY: Might be, then again might not be – I neither believe nor disbelieve in anything, right.

JOHN: Right.

RAY: Right. D'you believe in me? I believe in me.

JOHN: You're the only sod that does then, not even your mam and dad believe in you.

RAY: So d'you think there are, aliens here on earth now?

KENNY: Its like I said –

JOHN: Lot of aliens round here mate – Illegal
Aliens! Here Ken, you ever had an out of body experience in somebody else's body, you know – been someone else? No, I'm serious – go on, you can tell us – come on –

JOHN puts fist up his T-shirt, holds shirt taut, and thumps at it from underneath.

Urgh – I've got Kenny inside me.

RAY does as JOHN.

RAY: Alien.

JOHN: I've got Kenny inside me.

RAY: I've got Kenny inside me.

JOHN: I've got Kenny inside me.

RAY: I've got Kenny inside me.

KENNY: You know what you two want to do don't you.

RAY: What?

KENNY: Fucking grow up, the pair of you.

JOHN: Steady on Kenny.

RAY: We're only mucking about – honest. We won't take the piss no more, honest mate – here.

Offers hand.

JOHN: Yeah, honest.

Offers hand. KENNY does same JOHN and RAY pull hands away and pull faces.

Here, have you ever thought, what if you didn't exist?

RAY: What's in the fridge?

JOHN: If you were still here, but nothing you said or did had any effect.

RAY: Look in the fridge will you.

JOHN: Go on, try it.

RAY: Come on, you're nearest.

JOHN: Pretend you don't exist.

RAY: Do I have to?

JOHN: You don't exist.

RAY: I'm starving.

JOHN: Do it will you.

RAY: What for?

JOHN: Do it and I'll look in the fridge.

RAY: Alright. I don't exist.

JOHN: You don't exist.

KENNY: You don't exist.

RAY: Now what?

JOHN: You're not trying.

RAY: I'm trying.

JOHN: You don't exist.

RAY: I don't exist.

Enter CAROL.

CAROL: What's the matter with Ray?

JOHN: He doesn't exist.

RAY: I don't exist.

KENNY: You don't exist.

CAROL: Oh. Have you got any skins?

JOHN throws her cigarette papers.

Thanks.

Exit CAROL.

JOHN: But you're still here – Egoless. There's nothing.
Whatever you say or do makes no difference... You eat, you
smoke, you drink, you shag, but it makes no difference –
all you can do is sit and wait – you're stuck – it's pointless,
your life is pointless, it doesn't matter, whatever you do,
you're meaningless.

RAY drinks JOHN's beer.

What d'you do that for?

RAY: Do what?

JOHN: That's my beer.

RAY: What beer?

JOHN: Get me another beer – get us another beer will you. Get me a beer.

JOHN hits RAY over head.

RAY: What d'you do that for?

JOHN: Stop taking the piss.

RAY: You've been reading that French bloke again.

JOHN: Get me a beer.

RAY: Alright.

JOHN: You're useless, you are you can't even not exist without being a pain in the arse.

Scene 9

Kitchen. FRAN cutting cabbage. NEIL with bunch of flowers.

NEIL: I bought you some flowers.

I bought you some flowers.

NEIL puts flowers on table.

FRAN: Thank you.

He sits at table.

NEIL: Did you get my card?

FRAN: What card?

NEIL: The card I sent you.

He puts his feet on the table.

FRAN: You sent me a card – where from?

NEIL: What d'you mean where from, Scotland where from.

FRAN: You went to Scotland?

FRAN cuts off the top of the bunch of flowers.

Get your feet off my table. I said get your feet off my table.

She stabs at his feet.

NEIL: You're mad, you're fuckin' mad.

FRAN: I'm sorry – I missed. Did you have a nice time.

NEIL: No it rained.

FRAN: So you had something to talk to each other about.

NEIL: Who?

FRAN: Nellie – you and Nellie.

NEIL: Lottie.

FRAN: Get out.

NEIL: You, you get out, get out of my bloody head.

FRAN picks up knife.

Go on then.

FRAN: Get out.

NEIL: Go on.

FRAN: Get out.

NEIL: Go on.

FRAN: You've never felt anything for anyone other than yourself have you... you think you can just... and then turn up
with a bunch of dead daffodils and expect me to be glad to
see you – you take everything and give nothing.

She puts down the knife. Enter RAY.

RAY: That smells good – who's cooking?

Exit FRAN.

You're back then.

NEIL: Yeah.

RAY: Good was it? I like Scotland – it's like being in another
country.

NEIL: Yeah.

RAY: Wouldn't mind living there only it's so far away. I once
drove a lorry up to Inverness me and this bloke – we

bought these green sunglasses and got stoned driving through the mountains. It was brilliant.

Enter JOHN, carrying a tool bag.

JOHN: Oh, hello Neil – how did it go then?

NEIL: Yeah great.

Exit NEIL.

JOHN: What's up with him?

RAY: Dunno.

JOHN: You cooking?

RAY: No.

JOHN eats some cabbage.

RAY: You'll get worms.

JOHN: What do you know.

RAY: I'm telling you, you'll get worms.

JOHN: Put the kettle on.

JOHN puts tool bag on table.

RAY: Don't do that, you'll dirty it.

JOHN: So you can clean it – give you something to do. Who is cooking?

RAY: No one.

JOHN: I'm hungry.

RAY: Get a bag of chips then.

JOHN: When was the last time you cooked?

RAY: I don't cook.

JOHN: What do you do?

RAY: Alright I'll cook.

JOHN: You can't cook.

RAY: So I won't cook.

JOHN: You can't do anything, you're useless.

Enter FRAN.

JOHN: You alright? D'you want me to do anything.

FRAN: No, no thanks. I just... it's so... I wish... for once some-body would... they always, nobody ever... I don't believe it, that I've... I thought... never, never again.

RAY: I'll get some chips in.

Door slams offstage. Exit FRAN. Enter NEIL.

JOHN: I don't like you.

NEIL: Where's Fran?

JOHN: I've never liked you.

NEIL: I don't like you. Fuck off.

JOHN: You what?

NEIL: Fuck off.

JOHN: Say again?

NEIL: Fuck off.

JOHN hits NEIL.

Scene 10

Garden. KENNY on bonnet of van.

KENNY: Yeah, I've time travelled – I've still got the disclaim-er as a matter of fact – well, they don't like to take responsi-bility in case something happens, like you don't come back.

Scene 11

Front room. NEIL and FRAN.

NEIL: How are you?

FRAN: What do you want?

NEIL: How are you?

FRAN: How are you?

NEIL: Alright. How did you sleep?

FRAN: You're going out.

NEIL: Have a drink.

FRAN: I don't feel well.

NEIL: Have a drink.

FRAN: It's alright, I'll be alright you go out.

NEIL: You go out.

FRAN: I've lost my keys.

NEIL: Where did you lose your keys?

FRAN: I don't know.

NEIL: They'll turn up.

FRAN: Thanks. You'll be alright, your sort always are.

NEIL: What sort?

FRAN: I can't find my glasses.

NEIL: You've lost your glasses.

FRAN: No, my keys. Look in my pocket will you.

NEIL: Which pocket?

FRAN: That pocket.

NEIL: Your coat pocket. (*He looks in her coat pocket and pulls out some keys.*) Are these them?

FRAN: No. I've lost my keys, I can't find my glasses, I'm losing everything.

NEIL: When did you last have them?

FRAN: I don't know.

NEIL: They'll turn up.

FRAN: Thanks.

NEIL: I'm sorry.

FRAN: Thanks. You'll be alright. Maybe they're out in the hall – look on the hall table.

He goes out.

NEIL: (*Offstage.*) No.

Returns.

FRAN: Nothing.

NEIL: Nothing.

FRAN: I'm losing everything.

NEIL: It's alright, you'll be alright.

FRAN: What are you doing here?

NEIL: I wanted to see you –

FRAN: I don't want to see you.

NEIL: You've got some food?

FRAN: Where are you going.

NEIL: Get some food in.

FRAN: You're going to see her.

NEIL: You'll get some food in?

FRAN: I don't feel like going out.

NEIL: I'd best be off then. I'll ring you later.

FRAN: Yeah.

NEIL: Don't.

FRAN: What?

NEIL: Just don't.

FRAN: Don't what?

NEIL: I said don't. I just wanted to see that you were alright, that's all.

FRAN: Thankyou. You'd better go or you'll be late.

NEIL: Go to bed, lie down, have a drink, you'll be alright – get out. I'll ring you later.

FRAN: Yeah.

NEIL: Right. I'm sorry.

FRAN: I don't even like you.

NEIL: There's bound to be something on the telly.

FRAN: That's what you always say.

NEIL: Alright, so I won't say it.

FRAN: You'd better go.

NEIL: I'll speak to you later.

FRAN: Tonight.

NEIL: Yeah.

FRAN: You'd better go.

NEIL: I'll ring.

FRAN: No.

NEIL: I've said.

FRAN: Tonight.

NEIL: I'll speak to you later then.

FRAN: Where are you going?

NEIL: I have to go.

FRAN: Huh.

NEIL: What? I don't want to go.

FRAN: You've never been able to stay, there's always something else, someone else. You'd better go – I don't even want you to stay.

NEIL: I'll stay if you want.

FRAN: Do what you like.

NEIL: I'd like to get on a bus, the downstairs of an empty bus and go somewhere – nowhere in particular, just somewhere without paying the fare.

FRAN: That's because you're from Yorkshire.

Scene 12

Garden. KENNY starting up van.

KENNY: I get a thought, anything, a word, a look, it doesn't
matter and it gets stuck, goes round – I try to ignore it,
but it grows, a whole story round a word and everything
feeds it, then I go to bed and hang onto the fact that it's
not real, that what I'm imagining isn't real, that I've lost
touch with reality, but deep down there's some part of
me clinging onto it, it's the only thing that keeps me sane,
that stops me from going completely barmy. I don't know
what it is, I don't know why I get like this – it starts by
shutting it out, the thought, like he's trying to hurt me or
she's – I just want to wake up with the wind on my face,
fresh air, you know – I'm sick of paying money, I'm sick
of money, I'm sick of paying money to live in four walls –

Engine starts.

Scene 13

Front room. CAROL and SHARON.

SHARON: Oh God, I feel dead bad dead stupid –

CAROL: Sit down.

SHARON sits.

SHARON: I was in this shop trying on a dress, when I bent
over to pick up some shoulder pads and me knee just went
popped out – I couldn't help it – I felt bloody daft, stupid,
rolling about on the floor in this shop screaming and everybody looking at me like I'd gone mad, but I couldn't help
it, me knee just popped out – like that, out here it was, so I
pushed it back in – it's happened before but never this bad
– took me half an hour to walk here –

CAROL: Which shop was it?

SHARON: Du – Du – Du – Du – Du – Du it's on the High Street – and I bought the dress, well I had to after all that. Oh God I swear to God there's no fluid in that knee – bone on bone, I can feel it – go on touch it and see,

CAROL: Fran's gone to get you a bag of frozen peas.

SHARON: That's what the manageress said – she had a certificate in first aid.

CAROL: You can't go bowling like that.

SHARON: I'll sit and watch.

CAROL: You'd be better off staying.

SHARON: Oh, I get it.

CAROL: It's your knee I'm thinking of.

SHARON: It's you and Fran now is it?

CAROL: We'll have a drink when we get back.

SHARON: Don't let me get in the way of you having a good time.

CAROL: It's my only night off this week.

SHARON: Don't worry about me – just give us a cup of cocoa and a bag of frozen peas – I'll be turning summersaults by the time you get back.

CAROL: Don't be soft.

SHARON: It's not me that's soft.

CAROL: Look, I didn't ask you to break your leg.

SHARON: It's not broke.

CAROL: What's your problem?

SHARON: What d'you mean 'What's my problem', since when have you said 'What's your problem'. I've hurt my knee, alright.

CAROL: I'm only trying to help, there's no need to get irrational.

SHARON: Me irrational – bad karma, astral planes and faith healers, thats rational is it?

CAROL: Your mind's poisoned – no wonder you keep on getting spots, it's the poison exploding all over your body.

SHARON: Maybe I should go on a macro-biotic diet.

CAROL: Maybe.

Phone rings. SHARON stands and falls over.

CAROL: What d'you do that for!

SHARON: Don't shout at me.

CAROL: I'm not.

SHARON: I can manage on my own thanks.

CAROL: Sit down will you.

Phone stops ringing.

Open your mouth.

SHARON: What is it?

CAROL: Open it.

SHARON: What's in the bottle?

CAROL: Rescue Remedy.

SHARON: You what?

CAROL: Just do it.

CAROL squeezes some drops onto SHARON's tongue. Enter MICHAEL with large bag.

MICHAEL: Oh, sorry.

SHARON: No, don't go.

Enter RAY.

RAY: That the lot then?

MICHAEL: Yeah.

RAY: What you doin'?

SHARON: Carol's going bowling.

MICHAEL: What about food?

Enter JOHN.

RAY: Who was that on the phone?

JOHN: Sian.

RAY: Sian who?

JOHN: I dunno.

SHARON: You'd better go or you'll be late.

RAY: Who did she want?

SHARON: Don't worry about me.

JOHN: Roy.

RAY: Roy?

CAROL: I'm waiting for Fran.

RAY: Roy who?

JOHN: How should I know, he doesnt live here.

MICHAEL takes out an I Love My Father mug.

Kenny's got the van going.

RAY: Piss off.

JOHN: It's moving I'm telling you – he's off round the world.

SHARON: Did you get that for fathers day?

MICHAEL: No.

RAY: Here, I didn't know you had a kid.

MICHAEL: Yeah – six – China.

RAY: Big country – that where she lives?

MICHAEL: With her mother.

SHARON: China, that's a nice name.

Enter FRAN.

FRAN: They didn't have peas, I could only get cauliflower –

RAY: Just showing Michael round.

SHARON: You'd better go or you'll be late. Thanks for the cauliflower.

CAROL: I'll leave you the bottle.

SHARON: Great we'll have a party.

CAROL: See you later.

RAY: Yeah.

Exit FRAN and CAROL. Enter KENNY.

KENNY: Are you coming or what? Well?

RAY: Where are we going?

KENNY: I don't know – everywhere and anywhere.

RAY: Brighton.

JOHN: Bangkok.

RAY: Beirut.

JOHN: Basildon.

RAY: Brazil

KENNY: I've got a mate I want to see in Potters Bar first.

Exit KENNY.

JOHN: I'd better go up the bank.

RAY: Yeah put the rent in.

JOHN: All of it.

RAY: Yeah, all of it.

JOHN goes to exit.

Here –

JOHN: What?

RAY: Don't forget to take a bag.

Exit JOHN.

You coming round the world then?

MICHAEL: No.

SHARON: Not for me thanks, I've got a cat.

Exit RAY.

You're moving in then.

MICHAEL: Yeah. How's the knee?

SHARON: Fine – I've got Rescue Remedy. You're stopping in then.

MICHAEL: Yeah. I'll make some tea.

SHARON: Looks like rain.

MICHAEL: Yeah.

SHARON: We'll stop in together then.

MICHAEL: Yeah.

THE END

BAD COMPANY

Characters

BILLY HAYES
PAUL TURNER
SHIRLEY
STEVEN
MARY
NICKY TREDWELL
SHIRT
IAN SMITH

The play takes place in a northern seaside resort (Scarborough).

Time: the present during the summer.

If necessary an interval can be placed between Scene 15 and Scene 16.

Bad Company was given its first stage performance as a studio production by the Royal National Theatre Studio, on the 14th of December 1990, with the following cast:

BILLY HAYES, Paul Wyett
PAUL TURNER, John Hannah
SHIRLEY, Angela Clarke
STEVEN, Nicolas Tennant
MARY, Julia Ford
NICKY TREDWELL, Wayne Foskett
SHIRT, Mathew Wait
IAN SMITH, Jonathan Firth

DIRECTION: Paul Miller
DESIGN: Aldina Cunningham

Bad Company was later performed by the London Stage Company at the Bush Theatre, London, in the revised version printed here, on the 8th February 1994, with the following cast:

BILLY HAYES, Paul Wyett
PAUL TURNER, Kemal Sylvester
SHIRLEY, Nicola Sanderson
STEVEN, Nicolas Tennant
MARY, Suzanne Hitchmough
NICKY TREDWELL, Gary Sefton
SHIRT, Mark Petrie
IAN SMITH, Stuart Laing

DIRECTION: Paul Miller
DESIGN / LIGHTING DESIGN: Jane Barwell
LIGHTING DESIGN: Sacha Brooks
Produced by Howard Slone and Charlotte Barslund

Notes for *Bad Company*:
Any music used should be contemporary and drawn from the pop charts.

Scene 1

The beach. PAUL and BILLY are playing football. PAUL, stripped to the waist and barefoot, picks up the ball and bounces it like a basketball.

BILLY: You can't do that.

PAUL: See that girl.

BILLY: It's handball.

PAUL: She's giving us the eye.

BILLY: Penalty!

PAUL: She is.

    BILLY sits.

BILLY: Three and in or I'm not playing.

PAUL: She's still looking.

BILLY: I'm gonna get a mountain bike. (*He examines his feet.*)

PAUL: She can't take her eyes off me.

BILLY: Oh yeah?

    PAUL looks out to sea.

PAUL: Just smell it will you.

BILLY: These shoes are killing me.

PAUL: Go on.

BILLY: My feet hurt.

PAUL: Go on.

BILLY: I think they're swollen.

PAUL: Take your shoes off.

BILLY: I don't want to.

PAUL: Stop complaining then.

BILLY: Alright. (*He takes his shoes off.*)

PAUL: Look at it. See that rock over there? I had Lee Shipley behind that rock.

BILLY: Oh aye?

PAUL: I bloody did.

BILLY: They are, they're swollen.

PAUL: She was out of her brain on shoe polish.

BILLY: You bloody didn't.

PAUL: You don't believe anyone's ever done it, not even your mam and dad.

BILLY: Look at them.

PAUL: Particularly your mam and dad.

BILLY: I've always had bad feet.

PAUL: Not anyone's mam and dad. Look at it, that's all I come back for.

BILLY: You've eaten all the chocolate.

PAUL: Throw us me T-shirt.

BILLY does so. He picks up a postcard.

BILLY: (*Reading.*) Dear Paul –

PAUL: Don't read that.

BILLY: Dear Paul –

PAUL: Come on.

BILLY: Dear Paul –

PAUL: Billy!

They tussle for the card. PAUL gets it. BILLY snatches it back.

BILLY: (*Reading.*) Dear Paul – sorry I missed you – hope you had a good journey – might be up in your neck of the woods next week – maybe see you – please write soon – love, J – kiss – kiss.

PAUL snatches the card back.

Don't think much of the picture.

PAUL: What's wrong with it?

BILLY: I could do better than that.

PAUL: You wouldn't know which end of the brush to use.

BILLY: Did you fuck her in London?

PAUL: Chuck us the ball walnut-brain.

BILLY: It's punctured.

PAUL: G'is it here.

> *BILLY throws the ball.*

> No it isn't. Come on.

BILLY: Alright. Three and in, you're in. (*He shoots at the goal.*)

> *PAUL saves it.*

> Shit!

> *PAUL plays basketball.*

> That's handball. Paul!

> *PAUL dribbles round BILLY.*

> I'm going.

PAUL: She's still looking.

Scene 2

SHIRLEY and STEVEN.

SHIRLEY: I don't want to.

STEVEN: Why not?

SHIRLEY: Because I don't.

STEVEN: Please Shirley.

SHIRLEY: I've told you.

STEVEN: Shirley.

SHIRLEY: Grow up will you.

STEVEN: Come on, it won't take long.

SHIRLEY: I know.

STEVEN: Just the once it happened, one time that's all and you said it didn't matter.

SHIRLEY: Well it wasn't worth crying about, was it? Any girl so much as looks at you for longer than half a second and you have to change your underwear.

STEVEN: It's only you Shirley, only you do this to me.

SHIRLEY: No.

STEVEN: I love you.

SHIRLEY: Don't be silly.

STEVEN: But I do.

SHIRLEY: You're working yourself up Steven. Mary's waiting for me.

STEVEN: Stuff Mary, I can't go back to work feeling like this.

SHIRLEY: You've had a bag of chips.

STEVEN: Why are you doing this to me?

SHIRLEY: I'm not doing anything to you. Look, I've got to go.

STEVEN: Shirley!

Scene 3

The beach.

BILLY: You wouldn't just leave?

PAUL: No.

BILLY: You would.

PAUL: I've only just got back.

BILLY: Yeah.

PAUL: I'm not going anywhere, I promise.

BILLY: If you do, you'll take me won't you?

PAUL: I might.

BILLY: You wouldn't just leave?

PAUL: No.

BILLY: Here, I've got a mate knows someone lives in London, Alison something.

PAUL: Oh yeah, I know her.

BILLY: Short, blonde hair, from Burniston, got married to a bloke down there.

PAUL: It's a big place Billy. Look at it.

BILLY: It's alright.

PAUL: Is it?

BILLY: What's wrong with it?

PAUL: I haven't got any money.

BILLY: I've got money.

PAUL: I don't your money.

BILLY: Alright.

PAUL: Look at her.

BILLY: She's alright.

PAUL: Can I come and stay at your place?

BILLY: Yeah – why?

PAUL: Just forget it.

BILLY: Why?

PAUL: Give over will you.

BILLY: But I've only got one bed.

PAUL: OK – we'll toss for it. Tails it's mine.

BILLY throws a coin.

BILLY: Bollocks. Why can't you stay at home?

PAUL: I can. Look at that will you, a cargo ship coming into the harbour.

BILLY: It's from Norway.

PAUL: How do you know?

BILLY: By the colours.

Scene 4

Café on the edge of the beach. MARY is waiting. SHIRLEY enters.

MARY: Where's Steven?

SHIRLEY: I don't know.

MARY: Don't talk to me about it then.

SHIRLEY: There's nothing to talk about. He's got a headache, alright?

MARY: Unusual for him.

SHIRLEY: What's that meant to mean?

MARY: Nothing.

SHIRLEY: There's nothing wrong with me.

MARY: Just as well.

SHIRLEY: At least I've got a boyfriend. Oh, don't go.

MARY: Like you say, at least you've got a boyfriend.

SHIRLEY: What's the matter?

MARY: Nothing.

SHIRLEY: Come on, what is it?

MARY: Nothing.

SHIRLEY: Men aren't everything you know Mary.

MARY: I know.

STEVEN enters.

STEVEN: Have you seen? There's a bloody great cargo ship just docked into the harbour.

SHIRLEY: And here we are, sat wasting our lives away. We could all go down and watch it for the day, that'd be a real thrill, wouldn't it Mary?

STEVEN: It's the biggest I've seen down there for years.

MARY: I thought it was a tanker.

STEVEN: And what would a tanker be doing here? It's a ship.

MARY: What difference does it make? Could be a flying saucer for all I care.

STEVEN: Because this a fishing port, a timber port, a trawler port, a grain port, that's what this place is – it isn't all stupid pleasure boats and trips round the bay and amusement arcades and ice cream parlours and chip shops and funfairs and donkey rides and candy floss and bloody visitors and Cannon and Ball at the Floral Hall!

SHIRLEY: What do you know about cargo boats?

STEVEN: My dad used to work on the cranes.

MARY: How is your dad?

STEVEN: Alright – we haven't heard. D'you want a coffee? They're having trouble getting post off the rigs. Do you?

SHIRLEY: Oh, alright.

STEVEN exits.

MARY: I feel mean now.

SHIRLEY: His dad couldn't even spell the word "crane", let alone use one – just something to piss on after the pub.

MARY: His mother hasn't been out since he left her. I shouldn't have asked.

SHIRLEY: You're soft you. Now what?

MARY: Nothing.

SHIRLEY: Where are you going?

MARY: I'll send you a postcard.

MARY exits. PAUL and BILLY enter, PAUL carrying BILLY's football.

PAUL: You can't be trusted.

BILLY: I couldn't help it – I know that fruit machine, I couldn't lose.

PAUL: But you did.

BILLY: I hadn't put enough in.

PAUL: Go and get us a cappuccino.

BILLY exits. PAUL sits down.

What's up with Mary?

SHIRLEY: What's it to you.

PAUL: I only asked.

SHIRLEY: Looks like rain.

PAUL: Maybe.

SHIRLEY: Did it rain much in London?

PAUL: About the same.

SHIRLEY: Must've been exciting living there.

PAUL: Yeah.

SHIRLEY: I wish I could do that, just get up and go some-where else.

PAUL: Why don't you then?

SHIRLEY: Wouldn't know where to start – I couldn't just leave Steven. What did you do in London?

PAUL: Oh, you know – this and that. What you doin' tonight?

SHIRLEY: Dunno yet.

PAUL: Corner of Trinity Road, eight-thirty.

SHIRLEY: You what?

PAUL: Don't be late, I'm not waiting.

STEVEN enters with drinks.

STEVEN: Here we are then.

SHIRLEY: I wanted a cappuccino.

STEVEN: You've got coffee now.

PAUL: You can have mine when it comes.

STEVEN: The prices, they should have two prices – one for visitors and one for the locals.

PAUL: Did you see Billy?

STEVEN: Yeah, he's kicking shit out the fruit machine.

PAUL: Shit.

PAUL exits.

STEVEN: What did he want?

SHIRLEY: We were just talking.

STEVEN: I would've got cappuccino if you'd said.

SHIRLEY: This'll do now.

MARY enters.

MARY: Where's Paul and Billy?

STEVEN: One armed bandits. (*He squints his eye and jerks his wrist up and down.*)

SHIRLEY: Steven!

STEVEN: Just trying to put a smile on Mary's face.

NICKY TREDWELL and SHIRT enter. They sit at another table.

There's Nicky Tredwell and Shirt.

MARY: That's it, I'm going.

STEVEN: (*Shouting.*) Hello Nicky – how's it going then?

NICKY: Reet enough. Now then Mary.

PAUL and BILLY enter.

BILLY: It wasn't my fault – the machine's rigged.

PAUL: Well why put money in it then?

SHIRLEY: Sit down Mary.

STEVEN: Did you know, Shirt's been done for breakin' and entering.

MARY: He hasn't, has he?

SHIRLEY: That's what he says.

STEVEN: He has n' all. Haven't you Shirt?

SHIRT: You what?

STEVEN: They caught him in the carpet department of Boyes. He set off the alarm, so he rolls himself up into this great shag pile and waits, thinking he's safe like, but they brought dogs and sniffed him out.

MARY: I'm going.

BILLY: I'm thirsty.

SHIRLEY: You're staying.

STEVEN: Well I nearly pissed me'sen when I heard about it.

PAUL: It's your own fault, you beat up the fruit machine, the manager kicks us out, we don't have anything to drink.

STEVEN: God you lot are miserable.

BILLY: I'll have this one. (*He picks up a coffee off the table.*)

MARY: No, don't...

BILLY drinks.

That's Nicky Tredwell's – he was here earlier.

BILLY: Cheers Nicky.

SHIRLEY: You didn't talk to him, did you?

MARY: No.

SHIRT: If I get sent down, will you come and visit me?

NICKY: No.

SHIRT: Me mam said she will.

NICKY: Well she would.

STEVEN: Why did you leave London?

PAUL: I'm on holiday.

STEVEN: Wouldn't catch me living down there.

MARY: I'd like to live there, wouldn't have time to get bored in London.

BILLY: I like London.

STEVEN: You've never been there.

SHIRLEY: Neither have you.

BILLY: When we played Altrincham for the cup.

STEVEN: So when are you going back?

PAUL: I dunno.

BILLY: He's got a girlfriend down there.

STEVEN: Oh aye? Bit of a dark horse eh?

STEVEN pinches PAUL's bottom.

PAUL: Gerroff will you.

SHIRLEY: What's her name?

BILLY: Jay.

SHIRLEY: Pretty, isn't it?

IAN enters, wearing sunglasses. He sits at a table at the back and reads a newspaper.

BILLY: She might be coming to visit.

PAUL: Who says?

BILLY: Your postcard.

STEVEN: Here, what's Soho like?

SHIRLEY: Steven.

STEVEN: I'm just interested that's all. Is it like what you see on the telly – pouting girls, sat round nearly naked in shop windows, all sex shops, massage parlours, strip shows and prostitutes – you'd be alright Shirley, if you got stuck for a bob or two.

SHIRLEY: What's that meant to mean?

STEVEN: Nothing.

SHIRLEY: What about Mary?

PAUL: I'm going to buy a car while I'm up here.

BILLY: You haven't got any money.

STEVEN: You haven't passed your test either.

PAUL: So – who's gonna know?

STEVEN: What if you have an accident?

BILLY exits.

PAUL: We won't – you're coming with me.

STEVEN: You need someone who's qualified.

PAUL: You've had, lessons haven't you?

SHIRLEY: We could all go for a drive in the country.

MARY: Make a change from sitting round this place.

STEVEN: I've only got a provisional.

PAUL: You don't have to come.

STEVEN: Didn't say I wouldn't, did I?

SHIRLEY: Why do you always have to spoil everything?

STEVEN: I'll teach him to drive.

NICKY: I'd like to see someone jump off that top board with all their clothes on.

SHIRT: Yeah.

NICKY: Go on then – do it. Do it and I'll make it worth your while.

SHIRT: Oh aye?

NICKY: Aye – I'll give you a packet of fags.

MARY: Here, look over there will you.

STEVEN: (*Shouting.*) Hey Shirt, how's the carpet business going?

MARY: Flippin' heck, Shirley –

NICKY: (*To SHIRT.*) Sit down.

MARY: Why don't you just walk over and ask to sit on his lap?

SHIRLEY: You said to look.

STEVEN: Got any spare offcuts, me mam needs a new carpet.

SHIRT: I'll bloody twat thee one if tha don't watch it.

STEVEN: Oh aye, you and whose army?

SHIRT: I wouldn't need one.

NICKY: Just ignore the bugger and give us a fag.

STEVEN: Come on –

SHIRLEY: Belt up Steven and look over there.

STEVEN: Don't tell me what to do – bloody hell, what's Ian Smith doing here, thought he'd gone for good.

MARY: You think he'd say hello.

PAUL: Where's Billy gone?

SHIRLEY: He just hasn't seen us that's all.

STEVEN: Probably gone blind with too much –

SHIRLEY: Steven!

STEVEN: Too much reading, it's bad for the eyes.

MARY: Don't you ever think about anything else?

STEVEN: No, I love books me.

PAUL: Where's Billy gone.

SHIRT exits.

STEVEN: Where's blind dog Smith, been kidnapped by Indian take-away has it?

MARY: He's put his paper down, he's picking up his bag, he's coming over – how's me mascara look?

IAN crosses over to them.

IAN: Hello – didn't see you all sat there.

SHIRLEY: I'm not surprised with them things on.

MARY: You're back then?

IAN: Yeah.

STEVEN: What for?

IAN: I live here.

MARY: Good at college is it?

IAN: Not bad, you know.

STEVEN: You've gone skinhead?

IAN: No.

SHIRLEY: Like the gear.

MARY: Yeah, it's "Groovy".

SHIRLEY: D'you want a coffee?

IAN: No – thanks but I was just off.

MARY: You're different, ain't he Shirley?

IAN: How d'you mean?

MARY: You know, just different, it's the way you speak, it's different.

SHIRLEY: Funnny like.

STEVEN: Posh.

IAN: How's your dad getting on Steve?

STEVEN: Alright.

IAN: Still on the oil rigs is he?

STEVEN: Yeah.

IAN: Anyroad, I'd best be off.

MARY: Maybe see you later?

IAN: Aye.

MARY: We could all go for a drink.

IAN: Yeah, why not. See you around.

PAUL: Yeah.

IAN exits.

MARY: God you're rude.

STEVEN: Ponce. (*He gets up to go, taking BILLY's football with him.*)

SHIRLEY follows him.

PAUL: Where are you going?

STEVEN: For a walk.

SHIRLEY: To watch the tide come in.

STEVEN: Some of us have got to get back to work.

PAUL: Oh aye?

STEVEN: Aye.

STEVEN pinches SHIRLEY's bottom.

SHIRLEY: Steven!

STEVEN: Catch.

He throws BILLY's ball to PAUL. He spreads his hand over SHIRLEY's bottom as they go to leave.

SHIRLEY: Stop it will you.

They exit.

MARY: Oh no, I've still got the key to the linen cupboard – she'll kill us.

MARY exits. Silence. A ship's bell rings in the distance. SHIRT enters, soaking wet. NICKY puts a packet of ten fags on the table.

SHIRT: What's this?

NICKY: What's it look like?

SHIRT: You said a packet of fags.

NICKY: That is a packet of fags.

SHIRT: They're half smoked.

NICKY: I'll keep them if you want.

BILLY enters.

BILLY: I won, I hit the jackpot, I kicked it and the money just poured out. Where's everyone gone?

PAUL: To work.

NICKY and SHIRT come over to PAUL and BILLY.

NICKY: Which one of them are you shagging?

PAUL: What's it to you?

NICKY: This ball yours is it?

BILLY: No, it's mine.

PAUL: All of them. I'm shagging them all.

NICKY: You've been away, haven't you? There's someone been looking for you down the Harbour Bar. Said they knew you from London, didn't they?

SHIRT: Oh aye, London.

NICKY: Showed us this photo of you stood in front of a statue. Said they were only up for the day.

PAUL: What did you say?

NICKY: Why, what've you done.

PAUL: I've missed you.

Scene 5

Men's changing room at the swimming pool. PAUL is changing into trunks. IAN enters.

IAN: Excuse me...

PAUL: What?

IAN: Paul.

PAUL: Yeah.

IAN: How are you?

PAUL: Alright. What you doin' here?

IAN: Swimming. I tried ringing after the other day.

PAUL: We haven't got a phone.

IAN: Next door's.

PAUL: I'm not staying at home.

IAN: Your mam said. Thought you were in London?

PAUL: I am – I'm just here for the summer.

IAN: She didn't sound too bad.

PAUL: She's got pills. What did you want?

IAN: The hair dryer's broke.

PAUL: They're always broken.

   (*Together.*) Are you –

IAN: (*Together.*) Where do –

PAUL: You first.

IAN: Where do you live in London?

PAUL: All over the place – with a friend.

IAN: He must be loaded.

PAUL: Who says it's a he?

IAN: Just thought that's all.

PAUL: Are you still into all that political stuff or have you grown up?

IAN: What did you do in London?

PAUL: Grew up.

Pause.

IAN: D'you wanna go for a drink after?

PAUL: No.

IAN: We could go down the *Bell*.

PAUL: I don't drink there.

IAN: Whatever pub you want then.

PAUL: I said "no", didn't I?

BILLY enters in luminous Bermudas.

BILLY: Are you coming swimming or what? Hello Ian, you're home then, I heard you were.

IAN: Aye.

BILLY and IAN shake hands.

BILLY: Nice to see you.

PAUL: Goodbye then.

IAN: Yes, goodbye.

IAN exits.

BILLY: Are you coming or not?

PAUL: Yeah.

BILLY: There's a letter come for you. It's from London.

BILLY gives PAUL the letter.

Not a postcard is it?

PAUL: Did me mam bring it round?

BILLY: Yeah.

PAUL: What's she say?

BILLY: Nothing much, she was alright – just that someone keeps ringing for you and next door's getting pissed off. My phone keeps ringing n' all.

PAUL: Who is it?

BILLY: I dunno, they keep putting phone down.

PAUL: I'll be out in a minute.

BILLY: I'm under the diving board.

PAUL: Billy.

BILLY: Cool, eh.

BILLY exits. PAUL puts the letter in a jeans pocket and exits.

Scene 6

A pathway on the cliffside.

STEVEN: Anyway, I don't like him.

SHIRLEY: We're lost.

STEVEN: It's a shortcut, I promise, we'll come out over the South bay pool.

SHIRLEY: You're just jealous.

STEVEN: Don't have to worry about him anyway.

SHIRLEY: How do you know?

STEVEN: The manager called me over today, say's he reckons there's a full time job after the summer. Wants me to go over and help paint his house, as a favour like.

SHIRLEY: Bloody dogs.

STEVEN: Did you hear me?

SHIRLEY: Yeah, you're gonna paint someone's house.

STEVEN: I scratch his back, he'll scratch mine.

SHIRLEY: This manager, can he be trusted?

STEVEN: Yeah, course – he's a laugh, more like one of the lads. What's that going on down there?

SHIRLEY: Morris dancers.

Scene 7

The swimming pool. BILLY is sunbathing, PAUL drying himself with a towel.

BILLY: Move over, you're blocking the sun.

PAUL: Jesus, that's wicked – she shouldn't be allowed out with legs like that.

BILLY: Move will you.

PAUL: Put them on the side of a road and someone'd get killed.

BILLY sits up.

BILLY: Where?

PAUL: By the paddling pool.

BILLY: She's only about twelve.

PAUL: Don't be disgusting. The woman with her.

BILLY: She's ord enough to be your mam.

PAUL: I'm not looking at her face – it's the legs, look at them, I could get right up them, climb all the way up and eat her for dinner.

BILLY: Why don't you go over and ask her if you can borrow them for five minutes?

PAUL: I'd need all day.

BILLY: Go on, go and ask her if she wants a fuck.

PAUL: It's not the sort of thing you say to a complete stranger.

BILLY: You could take her to a hotel.

PAUL: I haven't got any money.

BILLY: She might have.

PAUL: I'm sunbathing.

BILLY: I'd keep an eye on the kid for you.

PAUL: No.

BILLY: Go on.

PAUL: No.

BILLY: Might make her 'oliday.

PAUL: What's that on your stomach?

BILLY: Where? (*He looks down at his stomach.*)

> *PAUL taps him on the nose as he does. Both lie back and sun themselves.*

Have you seen Rosemary Tredwell?

PAUL: No.

BILLY: Did she say anything?

PAUL: About what?

BILLY: I don't know.

PAUL: Then why ask?

BILLY: So she didn't say anything?

PAUL: What's there to say?

BILLY: Nothing. About you and her.

PAUL: What about me and her?

BILLY: Nothing.

PAUL: What's she been saying?

BILLY: I don't know.

PAUL: Come on, out with it.

BILLY: She said you tried to hypnotise her and it didn't work.

PAUL: It's not my fault she's got no imagination – stupid cow.

BILLY: You can't really hypnotise people.

PAUL: And levitate.

BILLY: I don't believe it. The whole body off the floor?

PAUL: You leave the body behind you idiot. I've left my body several times as a matter of fact.

BILLY: Where did you go to?

PAUL: Just into the world, that's all.

BILLY: What does it feel like?

PAUL: I can't describe it.

BILLY: Go on, try.

PAUL: I can't.

BILLY: I want to know.

PAUL: I can't.

BILLY: You were probably just dreaming.

PAUL: I could do it now if I wanted to.

BILLY: Go on then. Float up to the top board and back again.

PAUL: D' you want a Coke?

BILLY: You can't do it.

PAUL: I do it when I feel like it. Well do you or don't you?

BILLY: What?

PAUL: Want a Coke.

BILLY: I'll 'ave a lolly instead, strawberry.

PAUL exits. BILLY carries on sunning himself. NICKY and SHIRT enter.

NICKY: Come on Billy, haven't you got anything to say?

BILLY: What's there to say?

NICKY: About my sister.

BILLY: I don't know what you're talking about.

NICKY: You and my sister.

BILLY: I haven't done anything.

NICKY: I never said you had did I?

BILLY: No.

NICKY: You've been seeing her.

BILLY: No I haven't.

SHIRT: Are you calling him a liar?

BILLY: No.

SHIRT: Then he must be telling the truth.

NICKY: The changing rooms, now.

BILLY: I don't want to.

NICKY: Scared.

BILLY: No I'm not.

NICKY: Fight me.

BILLY: No.

SHIRT: He's scared.

BILLY: I don't believe in it, I don't believe in fighting.

SHIRT: Is that why you wear a cross?

BILLY: It's God.

SHIRT: He believes in God.

NICKY: Shut up. Do you go to church?

BILLY: No – I don't think you have to. I mean, if you don't go to church it doesn't mean you don't believe in Him, doesn't mean there isn't a God.

NICKY: Come on, leave him alone.

SHIRT: You what?

NICKY: I said leave him.

PAUL enters with a lolly and an ice-cream.

PAUL: What do you want?

NICKY: Listen, you queer bent bastard, tell him to leave my sister alone.

PAUL: What for?

NICKY: No reason.

PAUL: What's all the fuss about then?

NICKY: Nothing.

PAUL: Go home Billy.

BILLY: Why?

PAUL: Go home will you.

BILLY takes his lolly and exits.

NICKY: Think you're clever don't you.

PAUL: No.

NICKY: Been to London.

PAUL: So?

NICKY: Tell him to leave my sister alone, she's already spoken for – right.

PAUL: He hasn't been anywhere near her.

NICKY: How do you know?

PAUL: Because he hasn't.

NICKY: Tell him I don't like his face either.

PAUL: Don't go out with him then.

NICKY: Who's been seeing my sister?

PAUL: How the bloody hell should I know. Could be anyone.

NICKY: What's that mean?

PAUL: Nothing.

NICKY: What you sayin' about my sister?

PAUL: Nothing.

NICKY: Don't talk about my sister like that.

PAUL: Like what?

NICKY: Like that.

PAUL: What?

NICKY: Stop takin' the piss.

PAUL: I'm not.

NICKY: You are.

PAUL: I'm not.

NICKY: Bloody are.

PAUL: I'm not.

NICKY: Bloody are.

PAUL: Bloody not.

NICKY: Bloody are!

> *PAUL sticks his ice cream in NICKY's face. PAUL and NICKY fight.*
> *SHIRT joins in. BILLY and IAN enter. They join in.*

Scene 8

SHIRLEY and STEVEN

STEVEN: So where were you?

SHIRLEY: Out.

STEVEN: Out where?

SHIRLEY: Just out that's all.

STEVEN: What, on your own?

SHIRLEY: I went to the bingo.

STEVEN: You hate the bingo.

SHIRLEY: Where the bloody hell are we Steven?

STEVEN: Over the Spa.

SHIRLEY: I knew we should've stuck to the path.

STEVEN: It's a shortcut I'm telling you. Hang on –

He grabs SHIRLEY by the arm.

SHIRLEY: What?

STEVEN: You don't like the bingo.

SHIRLEY: Let me go will you. I wasn't with anyone, right.

STEVEN: Right. You smiled.

SHIRLEY: Oh, don't be soft.

STEVEN goes to kiss her.

No.

STEVEN: Come on.

SHIRLEY: We're lost.

STEVEN: Go on.

They kiss.

SHIRLEY: Stop it will you.

STEVEN: What?

SHIRLEY: Breathing in me face like that.

STEVEN: I can't help it, it's you – you get me going.

SHIRLEY: Suck on a mint then.

STEVEN: You've got beautiful lips.

SHIRLEY: Give over.

STEVEN: No, honest you have.

They kiss.

SHIRLEY: Stop looking at your watch.

STEVEN: I never.

SHIRLEY: I saw you.

STEVEN: Just a bit pushed for time that's all – gotta get back for the three-thirty from Newbury.

SHIRLEY exits.

Shirley.

Scene 9

BILLY's flat/bedsit. IAN is cleaning PAUL's bloody nose with cotton wool.

IAN: (*Shouting; off.*) We'll need more water.

PAUL: What are you doing?

IAN: Try not to speak.

PAUL: Don't tell me what to do – ouch, my nose.

IAN: I said not to speak.

PAUL: You hurt me.

BILLY enters with water and cotton wool.

BILLY: I've only got liquid detergent.

PAUL: I'm not a bloody germ you know.

IAN dabs at PAUL's nose.

Leave off.

IAN: Do you want this cleaned or not?

PAUL: No. (*He looks in the shaving mirror.*) I'm scarred for life, it'll never go down that won't.

IAN: You're magnifying it.

PAUL: Enjoying this aren't you?

IAN turns the mirror round.

IAN: It's just a cut that's all.

PAUL: Be different if it was your nose, we'd have had the plastic surgeon here by now.

BILLY: I get spots worse than that.

PAUL: Thanks Billy.

IAN: Stop going on will you, you're givin' me headache.

PAUL: I just got me head kicked in that's all, sorry about the fuss, I'll be right as rain by tea – get him an asprin Billy, doesn't matter about me.

IAN: You sound just like your mam.

PAUL: You leave my mam out of this. At least when she worked in a pub she only pulled the pints.

BILLY: You'd be in hospital but for him.

PAUL: So?

BILLY: I think you should say thank you.

PAUL: Thank you. And what about me, don't I get any thanks?

BILLY: They weren't going to touch me.

PAUL: No?

BILLY: No. Told them I believed in God.

PAUL: You what?

BILLY: Said I believed in God.

PAUL: You're lying.

BILLY: I do.

PAUL: You're telling me I got this for nothing? That Nicky Tredwell left you alone because he's soft in the head about God?

BILLY: Just as you came, they were going.

PAUL: Where to, church? Where are you going?

BILLY: To get some disinfectant.

PAUL: No, don't go.

BILLY: I want to.

BILLY exits.

IAN: Your hair's shorter.

PAUL: I've been disfigured.

IAN: Come here, I'll give it another wipe. I said come here.

PAUL does as he is told.

God you're stubborn. Short hair suits you. Remember that time you had your hair shaved and they made you wear a tin helmet to school till it had grown back?

PAUL: So?

IAN: I just remembered that's all.

PAUL: My eyes hurt.

IAN: Sit down.

PAUL: I want to stand up.

IAN: Stand up then.

PAUL: Stop telling me what to do, you're always telling me what to do.

IAN: Sorry.

PAUL: And don't apologise.

IAN: I'll go if you want.

PAUL: Piss off. Throw us me jeans. Just give us me jeans.

IAN picks up PAUL's jeans. The letter drops out. IAN throws PAUL the jeans.

And the letter.

IAN looks at the letter.

Give it here will you.

IAN gives PAUL the letter. PAUL puts the letter in his jeans pocket.

IAN: What are you getting dressed for? It's from London. You don't have to get dressed.

PAUL: I'll hit you if you don't stop it. Where are my shoes?

IAN: Going somewhere?

PAUL: I just want to know where my shoes are that's all.

> *IAN throws PAUL his shoes.*

> Ta. (*He puts his shoes on.*)

IAN: From a friend is it? Your letter.

PAUL: Don't start right, just don't start.

IAN: I'm not starting anything, I'm only asking –

PAUL: Don't, I said don't.

IAN: Why don't you stop feeling so bloody sorry for yourself and do something for once.

PAUL: Yeah. The only person you've ever loved is yourself. You walk round with a mirror forever held up to your face. (*He holds out the shaving mirror to IAN.*) Go on, take it.

IAN: I have to go.

PAUL: Yeah.

IAN: Come on, I'll buy you a drink.

PAUL: No.

Scene 10

BILLY's flat. BILLY is holding a letter over the spout of a boiling kettle, trying to steam it open. The door bell rings. It rings again, long and insistent.

BILLY: Shit. (*He puts the letter down, goes to answer the door and leaves the kettle boiling.*)

Scene 11

Night-time. PAUL and SHIRLEY.

PAUL: On a clear night you can see for miles, round the coast in either direction.

SHIRLEY: Pity about the fog.

PAUL: It's beautiful.

SHIRLEY: Is that the lighthouse?

PAUL: You don't have to see something to know it's there.

SHIRLEY: Just as well. I'm short sighted. What's your girl-friend in London like?

PAUL: Alright.

SHIRLEY: Is she pretty?

PAUL: Yeah, suppose.

SHIRLEY: What, don't you know?

PAUL: She's pretty, yeah. If you wanted to kill yourself this is the bridge to do it off – you'd have a great view, all the way out to sea. I'd do it in broad daylight.

SHIRLEY: Is that how I make you feel?

PAUL: Shout something.

SHIRLEY: No.

PAUL: Go on.

SHIRLEY: Someone might come.

PAUL: You can do anything you want up here.

SHIRLEY: What do you want to do?

PAUL: Chuck you off this bridge.

He tries to pick her up.

SHIRLEY: No don't, put me down.

They kiss. She pulls back.

PAUL: What's wrong?

Scene 12

BILLY's flat: the same setting as at the end of Scene Ten. The kettle is still boiling. BILLY and IAN enter. BILLY runs over and turns the kettle off. He burns his hand.

BILLY: I was just making a cup of tea.

IAN: Run it under some cold water.

BILLY exits. IAN picks up the letter and looks at it. BILLY enters.

BILLY: It's Paul's.

IAN: You've spilt water on it.

BILLY: I was making a cup of tea.

IAN: Show me your hand.

BILLY shows him.

BILLY: It's from London.

IAN: Must be important. What did he do in London?

BILLY: Dunno. He's taking me back with him. He didn't say when he'd be back.

IAN: I was just passing. There's hardly room to swing a cat in here – he could stay with his mum and dad.

BILLY: They don't get on – he thumped his dad, something to do with his mam I think. I get lonely, I like living with someone.

IAN: Show me your hand again.

BILLY does so.

You've got nice hands.

BILLY: I wear gloves a lot. I have to, I'm on jam doughnuts. You won't tell Paul about the letter. (*He takes the letter from IAN.*)

PAUL enters. BILLY puts the letter in his pocket.

IAN: I was just passing. How's the nose?

PAUL: Alright.

BILLY: I'll make us a cup of tea eh.

IAN: Billy was just sayin' you're takin' him back to London with you when you go. (*He pauses.*) I'll maybe see you then.

PAUL: Maybe.

IAN goes to leave.

Give us a ring tomorrow.

IAN exits.

BILLY: How long's he back for?

PAUL: I dunno.

BILLY: Anyroad, better get to bed – I've gotta be up early.

PAUL: What time d'you finish?

BILLY: Three.

PAUL: See you down the caff then.

BILLY: Yeah, alright.

PAUL: You have the bed tonight. I'll make do with the couch.

BILLY: I don't mind.

PAUL: Have the bed Billy.

BILLY: Alright.

PAUL: Here, there's nothing in you and Rosemary Tredwell is there?

BILLY: What d'you think I am, stupid?

PAUL: Night then.

BILLY: Night.

BILLY exits. PAUL takes out a letter from his jeans pocket and opens it. A ten pound note drops out. He pockets it and reads the letter. Then he turns on the radio. Pop music is heard. He picks up the phone and dials.

PAUL: (*Softly.*) Hello, Jim?... It's me... Me... No, I'm not in London... Listen... A radio... I dunno, soon... I told you... Listen... yeah, I got the letter... No, I don't want you to send me the train fare... Listen to me will you. I don't want you to write anymore... Because I don't... No, don't ring, you can't – I'm not at that number anymore –

Loud slam of a door. PAUL slams down the receiver and burns the letter. BILLY enters with a glass.

BILLY: What's that burning?

PAUL: Nothing, just me fag caught on a bit of paper that's all.

BILLY: You wanna give up smoking you do, it's bad for you.

PAUL: Yeah.

BILLY: It is.

PAUL: I know.

BILLY: Next door are at it again.

PAUL: Yeah.

BILLY: I'll get a glass of water then.

The phone rings.

Who's that?

PAUL: I don't know, leave it.

BILLY: Might be important.

PAUL: Leave it – they'll ring back if it is.

The phone keeps ringing. BILLY answers it.

I'm not here.

BILLY: Hello? Hello – is anyone there? (*He puts the phone down.*)

PAUL: Who was it?

BILLY: I dunno, they put phone down.

Scene 13

The cliffside. IAN enters, running. PAUL enters.

PAUL: I give up.

IAN: Come on.

PAUL falls to the ground.

You smoke too much.

PAUL: It's the air, I'm not used to all this air. Anyway I
touched you.

IAN: No you never.

PAUL: I did.

IAN: You didn't.

PAUL: I did.

IAN sits next to PAUL. PAUL tags him and jumps up.

IAN: Right.

PAUL: And no cheating this time.

IAN: I don't cheat.

IAN chases PAUL. They dodge and swerve.

PAUL: You and that bloke – you never did, did you? Both at the same time?

IAN: One after the other.

PAUL: You dirty bugger.

IAN: You're going to pay.

PAUL: For what?

IAN: Everything.

IAN brings PAUL down with a rugby tackle.

PAUL: Cheat, that's cheating, you're only meant to touch. You always did cheat that's how come you got to that school.

IAN: Have you ever thought about dying?

PAUL: Fuck off. What – what you laughing at?

IAN: You – you're bloody ugly.

They both laugh.

PAUL: So what am I going to pay for?

IAN: I don't know, what have you done?

BILLY enters.

BILLY: I love the smell of rubber. Can you smell it?

PAUL: Let's have a look at your forehead. Come on show us. Screw up your face.

IAN screws up his face and PAUL feels the lines on his forehead.

BILLY: Copper says people have been coming from all over.

IAN: (*To PAUL.*) Give over.

BILLY: You can see right inside – half the front room just gone, slipped, slipped down the cliffside and into the sea. There's a sideboard smashed into a tree half way down and sheets, a load of white sheets everywhere.

IAN: It won't be long before all this has gone and people will look back and say "They were cavemen, fucking cavemen".

PAUL: Got any sweets Billy?

IAN: It's over.

PAUL: What's this?

BILLY: I like Black Jacks.

IAN: It's all slipping away.

BILLY: Want a goodie? Come on, let's see if we can get any nearer.

PAUL: Get a better view on the telly.

BILLY: You're not coming then? So you're staying? I'll see thee later.

BILLY exits.

PAUL: I want a car.

IAN: What for?

PAUL: I'd just get in it and drive anywhere. I wouldn't stop till I had to, then I'd turn around and just keep on going.

IAN: You wouldn't get a mile before you killed yourself.

PAUL: I can drive.

IAN: Oh aye?

PAUL: Yeah.

IAN: Get off.

PAUL: What's slipping away?

IAN: Nothing.

PAUL: It's only a bloody hotel you know.

IAN: We did you know – he went first while I waited at the foot of the bed, then when he finished I took over.

Scene 14

The café. MARY is waiting. NICKY and SHIRT enter. SHIRT carries a bunch of flowers.

NICKY: Hello Mary.

MARY: There's someone sitting there.

NICKY: You never had to wait for me Mary.

MARY: Who says I'm waiting?

> *NICKY and SHIRT sit. SHIRT puts his feet up on the table.*

NICKY: Behave yourself.

> *SHIRT takes his feet off the table.*

SHIRT: Scared someone might think you're still going out with him?

MARY: Doesn't bother me Nicky Tredwell.

NICKY: G'ez another coffee Shirt.

SHIRT: You've got one.

NICKY: So? I want another.

SHIRT: I haven't got any money.

MARY: Nice flowers.

SHIRT: They're for me mam – d'you think she'll like them?

> *SHIRLEY and STEVEN enter.*

NICKY: See you later.

> *NICKY and SHIRT move to another table.*

STEVEN: I wouldn't go if I didn't have to.

SHIRLEY: I'm not stopping you am I?

STEVEN: I don't want to go.

SHIRLEY: Don't then.

MARY: If you two are gonna argue I'm going.

SHIRT: D'you think she'll like them?

NICKY: No.

STEVEN: Shirley.

SHIRLEY: Yes Steven.

STEVEN: What are you gonna do tonight then?

SHIRLEY: I don't know, wash me hair.

MARY: I wish something'd just happen, something big like an earthquake.

SHIRLEY: You're always bored you.

MARY: That's because everything's boring.

STEVEN: I'm never bored me.

SHIRLEY: Shut up Steven.

NICKY: Thought you didn't have any money?

SHIRT: I don't – I found them.

NICKY: Oh yeah?

SHIRT: Yeah, outside a shop.

MARY: We could go and see a play.

SHIRLEY: What for?

MARY: It'd be different – we could go to the one on Valley Bridge, I've always wanted to go there.

SHIRLEY: I've been, we went with the school.

MARY: I never did. What was it like?

SHIRLEY: Alright – it was something about dead posh people without any scenery, then they took us to see Orville the Duck at the Futurist and we had a really good laugh.

MARY: Come on let's go, we could get dressed up and make a night out of it.

STEVEN: Yeah.

SHIRLEY: Thought you were painting your boss's house?

STEVEN: So, doesn't stop you from going does it?

MARY: Come on, it'll be fun.

STEVEN: What else are you going to do?

SHIRLEY: Go for a drink with Tom Cruise.

NICKY: You haven't told her yet have you?

SHIRT: No.

NICKY: She'll hit the fuckin' roof, use your gob as a vase for those flowers, you'll need plastic surgery when she's done.

SHIRT: Yeah – but I think she'll like them.

PAUL and IAN enter. NICKY and SHIRT exit.

MARY: We're going to the theatre tonight, to see a play.

PAUL: Oh aye?

SHIRLEY: It's not decided.

IAN: What are you going to see?

MARY: Whatever they've got on I suppose.

IAN: You want to ring first, they might be booked out.

STEVEN: I suppose you know all about it? They'll get in.

IAN: Might not.

STEVEN: Hard day at the library was it?

SHIRLEY: Steven.

STEVEN: Well, I bet he's never been.

MARY: Of course he has.

STEVEN: When?

IAN: A while back.

STEVEN: He hasn't been.

PAUL: What d'you want to go and see a play for anyway?

SHIRLEY: It's Mary that wants to go.

MARY: I'll go on me own, you don't have to come.

STEVEN: She wants to.

IAN: I was ten, me mam was doing the coats and I had to go with her, they sat me at the back with an orange and a packet of crisps – it was an amateur production of *Waiting for Godot* by Samuel Beckett.

STEVEN: Told you he hadn't been.

IAN exits.

MARY: I'll ring them. Don't fancy coming do you?

PAUL: No thanks. I've already got something on.

STEVEN: Oh aye, pretty is she?

PAUL: Yeah.

STEVEN: Must be short sighted then. Here, have you heard about Patsi?

MARY: This another of your daft stories is it.

STEVEN: No.

SHIRLEY: Yes.

MARY: I'll call you later.

STEVEN: Wait on, I'll walk with you. It's his parrot, it's left him – he goes home one night and there's a note stuck to it's perch sayin', "Get Stuffed"

PAUL: Get away.

MARY: I'm going.

STEVEN: Hang on – it's true, honest – the cage door wide open and a window smashed – he reported it kidnapped and came down the pub ballin' his eyes out, bloody woman, you could see why the parrot left –

MARY: Are you coming or not?

STEVEN: They say he dressed it in a tutu.

PAUL: So who wrote the note?

MARY: I'm going.

STEVEN: Alright, you've got no sense of humour you lot – miserable sods.

MARY and STEVEN exit.

SHIRLEY: He knows.

PAUL: What does he know?

SHIRLEY: He keeps going on.

PAUL: He doesn't know, he knows nothing.

SHIRLEY: Someone's told him.

PAUL: There's nothing to tell, we haven't done anything. (*He puts his arm round her.*) Don't worry eh.

IAN enters.

SHIRLEY: I'll see you later.

PAUL: Yeah.

SHIRLEY exits.

IAN: What's all that about then?

PAUL: All what?

IAN: He'll have you if he finds out.

PAUL: Finds out what? D'you think she fancies me then.

IAN: I'm telling you he'll have you.

PAUL: Shut up and have a fag.

IAN: You haven't changed have you.

PAUL: Have a fag.

IAN: I've given up.

PAUL: C'mon, let's go and see Ray, get some stuff and go up the castle.

IAN: We haven't got any money.

PAUL: I thought you had money.

IAN: Not enough for that.

PAUL: He'll give us some.

IAN: No he won't.

PAUL: Yeah he will, he's always flush in the summer Ray, he'll give us a joint.

IAN: I don't fancy it.

PAUL: What's up?

IAN: Nothing. Let's go swimming.

PAUL: You go swimming. How much money have you got?

IAN takes some change out of his pocket.

IAN: One pound sixty-three.

PAUL: Go an' get us a Kit Kat – I'll pay you back later, go on
– look at her pushing the pram.

IAN: The bloke's better looking.

PAUL: I'm not looking at him am I. Go on.

IAN exits.

(*He shouts.*) Get your'sen a Mars, if you like.

Scene 15

The beach at night. PAUL and BILLY.

BILLY: She's not coming.

PAUL: I'm going to buy a Ford Zodiac – I like the fins. Leop-
ard skin seats and big fluffy dice – what do you think?

BILLY: I don't think this is right, doing it behind his back like
this. She's still his girlfriend.

PAUL: It's her choice, she doesn't have to come.

BILLY: Why couldn't we have met her in a pub?

PAUL: I like the beach.

BILLY: Rosemary Tredwell didn't.

PAUL: Forget the dice, I'll have a nodding dog instead. She's
been asking for you.

BILLY: Who? What's she say?

PAUL: I think she fancies you.

BILLY: Well I don't want to see her.

PAUL: You should've given her one the other week when you
had the chance.

BILLY: Why didn't you? She's not coming. I don't know what

you see in her?

PAUL: Long legs, fishnet stockings, a tight little black leather mini skirt with a zip running up the back, riding all the way up to her knickers.

BILLY: She doesn't dress like that.

PAUL: You haven't seen her in bed.

BILLY: Neither have you.

PAUL: Haven't I?

BILLY: No. Liar.

PAUL: Up here, I've seen it all up here, I've shagged her a thousand times already.

BILLY: So why do you need to go out with her.

SHIRLEY enters, carrying her shoes.

SHIRLEY: What's he doing here?

BILLY: I'd best be off.

PAUL: Hang on. It's alright, he won't say anything.

SHIRLEY: Why, what have we done?

BILLY: Look, I don't want to cause any trouble.

PAUL: Shirley –

SHIRLEY: Don't touch me.

PAUL: I didn't, I just want you to feel better.

SHIRLEY: What do you think you are, a bottle of asprin?

PAUL: I don't understand, why did you come?

SHIRLEY: To watch an eclipse of the moon, that's what you said. You never go anywhere without him.

PAUL: He's my friend – you don't like it, go home.

SHIRLEY: What if he tells Steve?

PAUL: He won't, will you?

BILLY: Tell who, what?

PAUL: Come on, don't be angry.

SHIRLEY goes over to BILLY and gives him a long slow kiss on the lips.

BILLY: What was that for?

SHIRLEY: Paul.

BILLY: I've never seen an eclipse of the moon before.

SHIRLEY: You don't see anything, that's the point, everything just goes dark for a minute.

PAUL: It's not like that.

SHIRLEY: Come on, give us a smile – I'm staying aren't I? If you don't like it, go home.

BILLY: What do we do when it happens?

PAUL: We don't have to do anything – just watch it go red.

SHIRLEY: I should've brought me space suit.

BILLY: We could light a bonfire.

PAUL: Why?

BILLY: I dunno, burn summat, be like joining in – that's what they did in the old days isn't it?

PAUL: That's stupid.

SHIRLEY: He's no fun is he Billy?

She kisses PAUL on the cheek.

I'm sorry.

PAUL: You're embarrassing Billy.

BILLY: No she's not.

SHIRLEY kisses BILLY on the cheek and runs her hand through his hair.

SHIRLEY: He's got lovely hair our Billy, hasn't he?

PAUL: You're drunk.

SHIRLEY: Just a couple of gins that's all, with Steve before he went... This isn't right... I shouldn't be here... He's painting his boss's house tonight.

PAUL picks up one of SHIRLEY's shoes.

PAUL: Hey Billy, catch.

He throws the shoe to Billy.

Over here, come on.

BILLY and PAUL throw the shoe to each other.

SHIRLEY: No, don't.

PAUL: Watch out for the sea Billy.

SHIRLEY: Give me the shoe Billy.

PAUL: Come on Shirley, come and get it.

SHIRLEY dives for the shoe.

SHIRLEY: It's not fair, there's two of you –

PAUL: That's how you play.

SHIRLEY dives at PAUL. He throws the shoe to BILLY and grabs her. They roll over and over.

SHIRLEY: Stop it, I'm dizzy, there's sand in my hair, I'll be sick.

They stop. SHIRLEY is on top of PAUL. She laughs.

We can't leave Billy. (*She rolls off PAUL.*)

BILLY: I don't mind.

SHIRLEY: Besides, I want to see the eclipse. I 'ate the beach, I always 'ave, ever since I were a kid.

BILLY: Listen.

PAUL: To what?

BILLY: The sea.

SHIRLEY: I haven't got the right body for it.

PAUL: What?

SHIRLEY: The beach.

PAUL: Don't be soft, you look great.

SHIRLEY: I'm too fat.

PAUL: No you're not.

SHIRLEY: I am.

PAUL: You're not.

SHIRLEY: I am.

PAUL: She's got a smashing body 'asn't she Billy.

BILLY: Yeah.

SHIRLEY: You're just saying that.

PAUL: No I'm not – you look bloody great in a bikini.

SHIRLEY: Bet you say that to all the girls.

PAUL: No.

BILLY: He said it to Rosemary Tredwell the other week.

PAUL: No I didn't.

BILLY: Yes you did.

PAUL: Lying get.

SHIRLEY: He didn't?

Pause.

BILLY: He did.

PAUL chases BILLY. BILLY dodges and jumps on PAUL's back and rides him like a bronco.

Yeehaaaa!

SHIRLEY: Ride him Billy.

PAUL: Gerroff.

BILLY: Bring me the head of Alfredo Garcia!

PAUL: Stop it.

BILLY: See how the gringo devil squeals.

SHIRLEY: Let's bury him in the sand.

BILLY: Up to his neck.

PAUL: You're choking me.

SHIRLEY: And leave his head for the crabs to chew on.

PAUL flicks BILLY violently over his shoulder, throwing him to the ground.

PAUL: Clumsy bloody idiot, he was choking me.

SHIRLEY: He was playing.

She helps BILLY to sit up.

PAUL: That's his trouble, he never knows when to stop.

SHIRLEY: Leave him alone.

PAUL: Since when have you been his friend?

BILLY: I'm fine, really.

SHIRLEY backs off.

SHIRLEY: How much longer do we have to wait? It's cold, I'm cold – and that wasn't an invitation for you to put your mucky paws round me.

PAUL: Why don't you go for a swim Billy?

BILLY: We could all go.

SHIRLEY: And freeze to death.

BILLY: Come on, it'll be fun.

PAUL: Shirley's right – you go, we'll just sit here and watch, won't we?

SHIRLEY: Will we?

PAUL: Only if you want to.

BILLY: Once you're in you can't feel the cold.

PAUL: We don't want to Billy.

BILLY: It's no fun on your own.

PAUL: You can't force us!

SHIRLEY: There's no need to bite his head off.

BILLY: I'll go for a swim. (*He undresses down to his underpants.*) You won't go?

SHIRLEY: Of course not.

BILLY: If you do, you'll leave my clothes behind?

PAUL: Yes.

BILLY exits.

SHIRLEY: What did he mean by that?

PAUL: Don't ask me.

SHIRLEY: Funny you are – up one minute, down the next, like a Yo-Yo.

PAUL: I just don't like it here, that's all.

SHIRLEY: It was your idea.

PAUL: Anyroad, come the end of the season and I'll be gone – might go to Torquay.

SHIRLEY: What d'you want to go there for?

PAUL: They've got palm trees.

SHIRLEY: You're mad.

Pause.

PAUL: Have you ever been hypnotised? Lie down and I'll make you float. I can.

SHIRLEY: Get away.

PAUL: Just lie down and trust me.

She lies down.

SHIRLEY: And no funny business.

PAUL: Close your eyes.

SHIRLEY: They are. Now what? I can't keep them closed forever.

PAUL: Clench your fists tight, tighter, grit your teeth and screw up your face – till your whole body's tense, rigid –

SHIRLEY: It is.

PAUL: Now hold it.

SHIRLEY: It hurts.

PAUL: Good, now let go, let it all out, feel your body sinking into the sand... all that pain draining away... sinking... deeper and deeper... till there's nothing... nothing... nothing...

Silence. PAUL circles her body.

Shirley.

Silence. PAUL kneels and leans forwards to kiss her. SHIRLEY slaps his face.

SHIRLEY: Don't stop.

PAUL stands up sharp.

PAUL: You're floating... drifting... Count backwards from a hundred... there's nothing in your head... it's completely empty... Floating... all you can hear is the sound of my voice... forever... without words... floating... without pain...

Silence.

Shirley. Can you hear me Shirley.

Silence. PAUL kneels, puts his hands on her ribcage and rubs upwards to her breasts. He hesitates.

SHIRLEY: Don't stop.

He kisses her. She frantically undoes his trousers while he pushes her skirt up. After a while PAUL rolls off.

What's wrong?

PAUL: We can't.

SHIRLEY: Why not?

PAUL: There's no protection. I haven't got any.

SHIRLEY: It's alright.

PAUL: It's not safe.

SHIRLEY: Is it Steven?

PAUL: I think you should go home.

SHIRLEY: I'll be seeing you then.

PAUL: Yeah.

SHIRLEY exits. BILLY enters naked.

BILLY: Where's Shirley?

PAUL laughs.

Scene 16

The café.

MARY: (*Shrilly.*) "Don't talk to the guests Mary, it's rude", it's not as if I could, even if I wanted to, they're all Japanese. How dare she speak to me like that in front of everyone – she's never liked me. All I said was "Sianora".

SHIRLEY: Do you want this doughnut?

MARY: What were you doing last night?

SHIRLEY: Watching a video.

MARY: She's no right to speak to me like that.

SHIRLEY: It's her hotel.

MARY: Just because people take to me – she's like a block of ice. Guests are always giving me things, she can't stand it – these Japanese keep on leaving me presents.

SHIRLEY: Like what?

MARY: Nothing special. Tea-bags.

SHIRLEY: Tea-bags?

MARY: From Japan.

SHIRLEY: I wouldn't be jealous of that.

MARY: You can't buy them in the shops.

SHIRLEY: I'd rather have their money. You should get another job – I wouldn't like to change other people's dirty sheets all day.

MARY: Nobody's asking you to.

SHIRLEY: You should do what I do, people are always glad to see me.

MARY: Especially the men.

SHIRLEY: They book in, they book out, I smile and that's all.

MARY: It's not me – flirting with other women's husbands all day.

SHIRLEY: I don't flirt, I'm paid to smile: the bigger the smile the better the tip.

MARY: I couldn't do it.

SHIRLEY: No – it's not everyone can be a receptionist.

MARY: I'd feel daft – like one of those flippin' stupid donkeys over there – all dressed up with nowhere to go, silly great grin stuck on me face.

SHIRLEY: I don't feel like a donkey.

MARY: I wish I could just run away.

SHIRLEY: You could go to Birmingham.

MARY: I'd just go and I wouldn't stop.

SHIRLEY: That's where Steve's dad ran off to, the Black Country with Mrs Curran.

MARY: It's his mum I feel sorry for – after all those years and the man you love runs off with another woman.

SHIRLEY: She let herself go.

MARY: Fancy running away to Birmingham. I mean when you think about running away, it's to somewhere exotic, somewhere warm, somewhere exciting, not Birmingham.

SHIRLEY: It's probably all they could afford, about as far as their imaginations could stretch.

MARY: Have you seen Paul?

SHIRLEY: No.

MARY: I think he's quite exotic, the way he keeps going off.

SHIRLEY: Look at him over there, the one with the Union Jack shorts –

MARY: I quite fancy him actually.

SHIRLEY: He's got a face like a melted down wellington boot.

MARY: No he hasn't.

SHIRLEY: What d'you call them cheeks then? (*She sucks in her cheeks.*) Wouldn't catch me kissin' that, all those spots, catch blackheads.

MARY: Not off Paul you wouldn't.

SHIRLEY: What's Paul got to do with it?

MARY: I fancy him.

SHIRLEY: So why tell me, tell him – what do I want to know who you fancy for?

MARY: There's no need to get short.

SHIRLEY: You hardly know him.

MARY: I've known him since junior school.

SHIRLEY: You're wasting your time.

MARY: How do you know?

SHIRLEY: He's not your sort.

MARY: That's for me to decide. I don't tell you what to think about Steven, do I?

SHIRLEY: That's different, I don't pretend to love him. You're just soft you are, always falling in love, always getting hurt. You're too old for love.

MARY: That what you think is it?

SHIRLEY: Yeah.

MARY: Right.

SHIRLEY: Right.

MARY: I thought you were me mate.

SHIRLEY: I am, that's why I'm tellin' you. Where's Steven?

MARY: How should I know?

PAUL enters.

PAUL: Hello.

MARY: Hello Paul.

PAUL: I'll get a drink then. D'you want anything?

SHIRLEY: No ta.

MARY: Yes please – cappuccino, no sugar.

PAUL exits.

SHIRLEY: Gets right up my nose the way he goes on about having no money, no job – all he does is lie around on the beach all day – he's never had a proper job.

MARY: What about your Scott, when was the last time he had a job?

SHIRLEY: That's different, it's his nerves.

MARY: Oh aye?

SHIRLEY: Yeah, he's got a doctor's note.

MARY: What about that chip shop he painted?

SHIRLEY: No sugar, since when haven't you taken sugar?

MARY: I'm on a diet.

SHIRLEY: What for?

MARY: No, you're right – it's not me that should be watching me figure, is it.

STEVEN enters.

STEVEN: And how are my favourite girls tonight?

SHIRLEY: Belt up Steven, you're late and I'm going home.

STEVEN: What about the pictures?

SHIRLEY: Stuff the pictures.

PAUL enters with cappuccinos.

PAUL: Now then Steve.

STEVEN: Now then.

SHIRLEY: So, you're gonna talk to him all night are you?

STEVEN: No.

SHIRLEY: I thought we were going to the pictures.

STEVEN: You just said you were off.

SHIRLEY exits.

Shirley!

STEVEN exits.

PAUL: What's up with her?

MARY: Dunno. Thanks. What you doing tonight?

PAUL: Go for a drink with Billy.

MARY: You've caught the sun.

PAUL: Aye, there's been a lot of it.

MARY: It suits you. I haven't been to the pictures for ages. It's no fun on your own is it? Shirley and Steven are always going.

PAUL: You should go with them then.

MARY: I'd feel like a gooseberry – 'sides, you never know when they're going to have an argument. The last film I went to see was *Lethal Weapon II*, it were dead good. Have you seen it?

PAUL: Yeah.

MARY: They've got *III* on at the Opera House.

PAUL: Have they.

MARY: Yeah.

PAUL: I saw it in London.

MARY: Oh.

IAN enters with two bags of chips.

IAN: Here you go.

PAUL: Ta.

IAN and PAUL open the bags of chips.

IAN: D'you want one?

PAUL: Ah what –

MARY: No thanks.

PAUL: They've got vinegar on.

IAN: So?

PAUL and IAN eat the chips. Silence.

MARY: Hot isn't it?

PAUL: Too hot.

IAN: You could fry an egg on the bonnet of a car, like they do in the desert.

MARY: Who does?

IAN: The Army.

PAUL: Bollocks.

IAN: Don't you want them?

PAUL: They've got vinegar on, I don't like vinegar.

IAN: You should've said.

PAUL: You know I don't like vinegar.

IAN: You should've said.

PAUL: I didn't think I had to.

IAN: Here, have mine.

PAUL: I don't want yours.

IAN: Have them they've got nothing on.

PAUL: I like them with salt.

MARY: I'll see you later then.

PAUL: Where you going?

MARY: Work – I have to. Thanks for the cappuccino.

   MARY exits.

IAN: She fancies you.

PAUL: You know I don't like vinegar.

IAN: Give over will you for Christ' sakes, I'm not your bloody mam. Go and get another portion then, it's only a packet of chips.

PAUL: I'll make do with these.

IAN: If you don't like vinegar don't have vinegar.

PAUL: I'll eat these.

   They eat. Pause. PAUL pushes his chips away.

IAN: I'm thinking of going.

PAUL: What's stopping you?

IAN: No, I mean going away. We could go together.

PAUL: I'm on holiday.

IAN: Think about it eh.

PAUL: Pack it in.

IAN: What?

PAUL: Tellin' us what to do.

IAN: I know what you did in London.

PAUL: Yeah?

IAN: Yeah – there's someone down there.

>*PAUL screws up his chips.*

>Why won't you tell us?

PAUL: There's nothing to tell. (*He throws his chips away.*)

Scene 17

>*A pub. NICKY and SHIRT stand holding pool cues.*

NICKY: Your shot.

>*Pause.*

>Just do it will you.

SHIRT: I'm thinking.

NICKY: They don't respond to telepathy.

SHIRT: I can't decide which ball to hit.

NICKY: It doesn't matter.

SHIRT: Why not?

NICKY: Because you're a shit player.

SHIRT: Pool's not my game that's all, I can't work out the angles.

>*STEVEN enters. NICKY blocks his way.*

STEVEN: Shove off will you.

NICKY: Please.

STEVEN: I haven't got time for games.

SHIRT: Why, what's up?

STEVEN: Nothing.

NICKY: Need any help?

STEVEN: Just move will you.

NICKY: Lookin' for someone?

STEVEN: No.

SHIRT: Where's Shirley then?

STEVEN: Look you've got summat to say, say it or get out the way.

NICKY: Giving you a spot of bother is she?

STEVEN: No.

NICKY: Out for a drink on your own eh. Sit down, have a drink with us. Have you decided which ball to hit yet? Take a seat, doesn't cost 'owt.

STEVEN sits.

Not in a hurry are you. So, how's it going?

STEVEN: Alright.

SHIRT: You've snookered me.

NICKY: Just hit the ball will you. He's having trouble deciding which ball to hit. D'you like pool?

STEVEN: It's alright.

NICKY: I don't like it down South. Miserable lot, all out for their sen. I've been there. You can see it just by going on the Tube – nobody laughs. Up here we're different, we all stick together – one fights we all fight, one doesn't fight – we make him see sense. Don't go Steven.

STEVEN: I'm not.

NICKY: Good.

STEVEN: Why d'you pick a fight with Billy and Paul?

NICKY: Why not?

SHIRT: Just a friendly scrap, that's all.

STEVEN: It's been nice talking then.

NICKY: You've not heard anything about our Rosemary have you?

STEVEN: No – should I have?

SHIRT: I can't do it, there's not a ball I can hit.

NICKY: Go off the bloody cushion then. This is just between you and me right. She's foolin' around with someone and Paddy only just gone to Belfast. So if you hear of anything you'll tell us, won't you?

STEVEN: Yeah, course.

NICKY: I don't approve of that, fellas messin' round with other bloke's birds behind their back.

STEVEN: What you gonna do about it?

NICKY: What would you do if you found out Shirley was carrying on?

STEVEN: She's not.

NICKY: But just supposing.

SHIRT: Smart looking lass, lot of blokes I know wouldn't mind –

NICKY: Shut it eh.

STEVEN: I should knock his block off for even suggesting it.

NICKY: Just take your shot. But what would you do?

STEVEN: I'd kill the bastard.

NICKY: We could give you a hand if you like.

STEVEN: I wouldn't need help.

NICKY: Aye, but what if he had friends? That's what happened with Billy, his friends got in the way. Here, you don't fancy givin' us a hand do you – seein' how we'd help you out if you were in trouble?

STEVEN: No.

NICKY: Aye, mates of yours aren't they.

STEVEN: What, you think it's Billy?

NICKY: I dunno.

STEVEN: Why don't you just ask her.

NICKY: And you think she'd say?

STEVEN: Ask her if there's anything goin' on, ask her if it's Billy, ask her straight to her face, you'd know if she was lying.

SHIRT: And even if she said "no" it wouldn't prove anything would it.

NICKY: And we'd lose the element of surprise – she'd know that we know and likewise this fella. No, we'll just watch. See who she talks to, how she behaves, soon be able to tell who it is. Meanwhile I'm gonna thump Billy for it. So if you hear anything you'll let us know.

STEVEN: Yeah.

NICKY: And don't forget, if ever you need any help.

STEVEN: Aye, thanks.

STEVEN exits.

Scene 18

IAN and PAUL. IAN is lying on his back with his knees up. A bottle of cider is between them.

IAN: It doesn't matter –

PAUL: Oh no, you're not going to start are you.

IAN: Whatever position you're in, the whole world's spinning.

PAUL: Just shut up and look.

IAN sings.

IAN: I know all the words, just can't get them in the right order. (*He sings loudly.*) Whey-a-whey-hey!

PAUL: That's Corrigans those lights.

IAN: We could go for a game of bingo.

PAUL: I hate this place in winter.

IAN: Yeah, no Max Jaffa at the Spa or Little'n'Large to cheer us all up.

PAUL: He's dead now.

IAN: Who?

PAUL: Max Jaffa.

IAN: They're all dead.

PAUL: Just give us a drink.

IAN: If I said, right now, anything you want, you can change it, what would it be?

PAUL: I give in, what's the answer?

IAN: Close your eyes, imagine the world –

PAUL: Do I have to?

IAN: Go on.

PAUL closes his eyes.

What can you see.

PAUL: A room. A big room. With a door.

IAN: What can you see?

PAUL: The door.

IAN: What else?

PAUL: Nothing, it's dark.

IAN: Open the door.

PAUL: It's locked.

IAN: Turn on the bloody light then.

PAUL: The bulb's broke.

IAN: You're bloody useless you are.

PAUL: What if you don't want to change anything.

IAN: Here, have a drink.

They both swig from the bottle.

PAUL: What about the sea?

IAN: Take a saucepan –

PAUL: I always hate it when you get like this.

IAN: Come on.

PAUL: I don't want to.

IAN: You've given up.

PAUL: When you said a drink, I thought you meant a pint.

IAN: Why won't you argue with us?

PAUL: Because I don't understand what you're saying half the time.

IAN: Fuck off. See this arm – whose arm d'you think that is?

PAUL: I don't know, looks like yours.

IAN: That's what I thought for all these years – then the other day I looked down and they weren't my arms anymore.

PAUL: Whose are they then?

IAN: I looked down and I saw my father's arms hanging off me – don't you see – there's no escape, you can't just run away, it goes with you.

PAUL: I don't care – I don't give a fuck about anything. (*He takes out a lighter and holds his palm over it.*)

IAN: You need petrol if you're gonna do it properly.

PAUL: Yeah – you'd buy it for us'n'all wouldn't you.

IAN: Only if you give us the money.

PAUL holds his palm over the flame until he can't stand it anymore.

PAUL: Shit!

IAN: Let me see.

PAUL: Piss off.

IAN: Show me.

IAN grabs PAUL's hand and pours cider over it.

PAUL: Now lick it off.

IAN kisses PAUL. PAUL pulls away.

IAN: What's the matter?

PAUL: I don't want to.

IAN: Why not?

PAUL: Because I don't.

IAN: You've never not wanted to before.

PAUL: Yeah, well that was before.

IAN: So you don't want to?

PAUL: Yeah.

IAN: Doesn't bother me. Sit down will you.

PAUL: I'll be alright after I've, after...

IAN: After what?

PAUL: Just after. It's easy for you, you've always known what you are, what you wanted, but I'm different.

IAN: How?

PAUL: I like girls for a start.

IAN: Do you?

PAUL: Doesn't bother you what people think does it?

IAN: Not anymore, no.

PAUL: Can't do anything in this place, that's why I went to London.

IAN: What did you do down there?

PAUL: Made a film.

IAN: Come on. You'll like it, you know you will. You've liked it before.

PAUL: Fuck off will you and listen to me, you never bloody listen to me.

IAN: Alright, I'm listening.

PAUL: No.

IAN: Tell me.

PAUL: Stop telling us what to do.

IAN: I'm not.

PAUL: You do.

IAN: Sit down.

PAUL: I'll hit you.

IAN: Do what?

PAUL: You heard.

IAN: Sit down can't you.

> PAUL *cuffs IAN over the head.*

You hit me.

PAUL: I said.

IAN: Bloody mental you are.

PAUL: Yeah, runs in the family.

IAN: How is your mam?

PAUL: I dunno.

IAN: Doesn't anyone come round to see her?

PAUL: Like who.

IAN: Doctor, social worker, you know.

PAUL: You used to be clever before you went to university.

IAN: Is that why you're not stayin' at home, because of her?

PAUL: No. I got off at King's Cross and didn't know where the fuck I was, it was all just London – so I ended up working my way round the Monopoly board, asking for all the places I'd seen on telly. I was just like any other tourist, ended up in the West End. I had a toothbrush, bar of soap, pair of socks and a change of underwear. It was alright till the money run out.

IAN: How long was that?

PAUL: About two days.

IAN: Then what?

PAUL: I didn't have any money did I.

IAN: Didn't you sign on?

PAUL: What d'you give as an address, the Embankment?

Applied for a loan – to the Social like, for the deposit on a room – they wanted to know how I was gonna pay it back, so I said, "Instalments", the bloke laughed, he was alright really.

IAN: Where did you sleep?

PAUL: Anywhere – shop doorways, parks, squats, building sites, bridges, the Salvation Army give out sleeping bags. One night I went down Waterloo, the Bullring, a whole island sunk into the traffic, looks like summat out the Stone Age – bonfires, dogs, kids, smoke, drunks, people shouting, the old and the mad living in a cardboard box. And people just walk by, looking through you like you weren't there. One night were enough for me. I didn't sleep, always tired, always hungry, always soaked to the bone – one morning I got woke up with a hose pipe showering us down; they were cleaning the pavement, ready for people to walk on it. Anyroad... I was back at King's Cross one day... And this young fella comes up to us with a cup of tea...

IAN: Yeah?

PAUL: Yeah – and he give us his tea.

IAN: So?

PAUL: So I came home.

IAN: I don't get it – why did he give you his tea?

PAUL: I dunno, maybe he were a bit soft in the 'ead, I mean why else would someone give you summat for nowt? He invited me back to his place for the night. Nothing in it he says. It was a big house, all the rooms empty but for one. He says to wait, so I sit on the bed – then this old man comes in, puts a fiver down and takes off all his clothes. It was alright for a while – then one night I said "no", wanted to watch Laurel and Hardy on the telly instead – so they kicked us out. He was a grizzly ord bastard. I went down Piccadilly Circus and met up with some other lads; we had a good laugh. We hung round Soho mostly, in the pubs, picking up passing trade – old men, married men, young men, the world without his wife. I only did it for the money. Had a couple of girlfriends – nothing serious like.

IAN: What about your friend, the one you stay with.

PAUL: There isn't anyone.

IAN: So who's your letter from then?

PAUL: I don't know, I haven't opened it yet.

Scene 19

The Gents in a night-club. Music is playing in the background. BILLY is smoking. STEVEN enters.

STEVEN: Where's the party then?

BILLY: Dunno.

STEVEN: Cheer up, it 'asn't 'appened yet.

BILLY: Just trying to cool down.

STEVEN: What's up?

BILLY: Nothing.

STEVEN: Why don't you just tell me to bog off? Get it eh? Bog off from a bog.

BILLY: Yeah, funny.

STEVEN: Miserable sod. There's a funny smell in here.

BILLY: What smell? I can't smell anything.

STEVEN looks in the mirror.

STEVEN: If looks could kill I wouldn't be able to look in another mirror. (*He combs his hair.*)

BILLY: Yeah, like the shirt.

STEVEN: Frankie Boyds, got it half price in the fire sale – Nigel Sqires tried to burn the place down after they gave him the sack.

BILLY: Yeah, I heard.

STEVEN: Reet then, no point gabbin' in here all night is thee? I'm off to get caylied.

BILLY: Is Rosemary Tredwell still out there?

STEVEN: God you stink.

BILLY: High Karate.

STEVEN: That won't pull anything – what you need's one of these, (*He indicates the place on his trousers.*) johnny pocket – sends out the message, ready, willing, and prepared. What's that on your teeth?

BILLY: Where?

STEVEN: There.

BILLY: I can't see anything.

STEVEN: Open your mouth, wider.

STEVEN pops a Durex in BILLY's mouth.

STEVEN: Chew on that, it'll give you something to think about.

STEVEN exits. In the night-club, SHIRLEY and MARY are on the edge of the dance floor.

MARY: I feel so nervous.

SHIRLEY: Don't be, you look great.

MARY: What if he says "no"?

SHIRLEY: He won't. Don't give him the chance, just grab him by the hand and get him on the dance floor.

MARY: But when?

SHIRLEY: When you feel like it.

MARY: I don't feel like it.

SHIRLEY: Then don't.

MARY: Why are you always so negative?

SHIRLEY: What d'you mean, negative?

MARY: The opposite of positive. You know what I mean.

SHIRLEY: No, I don't.

MARY: If you think positively, that something's going to happen, then it will. But if you just stand about thinking negative thoughts, putting yourself down, thinking the worst all the time, then you can only expect the worst to happen.

SHIRLEY: Where d'you read that, back of a matchbox.

MARY: It's true. You've got to be positive about life.

SHIRLEY: D'you want another drink?

MARY: No.

SHIRLEY: No need to get like that.

MARY: I'm not getting like anything.

SHIRLEY: Hang about.

MARY: What?

SHIRLEY: So you're telling me, if I stand here and think that Phil Collins is gonna come through that door and ask me to marry him, he will?

MARY: You don't like Phil Collins do you?

SHIRLEY: Yeah, why not?

MARY exits.

Mary!

PAUL is on the phone in the night-club.

PAUL: Hello – hello – is anyone there? Can you hear me? I can't hear you – it's me, Paul – is anyone there?

Money runs out.

Shit!

IAN is by himself in the night-club. He is writing in a little black notebook. MARY joins him.

MARY: Have you seen Paul?

IAN: What?

MARY: Have you seen Paul?

IAN: No.

Pause.

MARY: What's that you're writing?

IAN: Nothing.

MARY: Can I have a look?

IAN: It's nothing.

MARY: I write things in my head. Poems while I'm working. Would you like to hear one?

IAN: Are they funny?

MARY: No, should they be?

IAN: No I just thought they might be.

MARY: Why?

IAN: I don't know.

MARY: You're not really interested are you?

IAN: I am.

MARY: Are you sure you haven't seen Paul?

IAN: I said didn't I?

MARY: No need to get shirty.

IAN: I'm sorry, I was just –

MARY: Why should they be funny?

IAN: You don't understand.

MARY: Don't I? You're a snob – write that in your little black notebook.

MARY exits.

PAUL: Hello – hello – bloody answer me will you, I need you to answer me – bloody phone! (*He slams down the receiver.*)

IAN joins STEVEN and SHIRLEY who are sitting at a table on the edge of the dance floor.

STEVEN: Didn't expect to see you here tonight.

IAN: I'm going tomorrow.

STEVEN: I'll get you a drink.

IAN: I've got an orange juice.

STEVEN: What's up eh? On the penicillin? You hear that Shirley, the professor's on the wagon.

SHIRLEY: Silly cow.

STEVEN: You what?

SHIRLEY: I said she's a silly cow.

STEVEN: That's no way to talk about your mother, is it prof?

SHIRLEY: Mary, getting worked up over Paul.

STEVEN: He's not worth it.

IAN: That's why she's in a bad mood.

SHIRLEY: She's been looking for him all night.

STEVEN: Funny that I haven't seen him since we got here – have you?

SHIRLEY: No. Please don't drink anymore.

STEVEN: It's Saturday night, besides I've got something to celebrate.

SHIRLEY: What?

STEVEN: I'll tell you later. So, back to university is it?

IAN: Not straight off, no.

SHIRLEY: What you celebrating?

STEVEN: Back to the bookworms.

SHIRLEY: Steven behave.

STEVEN: I'm only joking, he knows that – don't you prof?

IAN: Yeah.

STEVEN: I wouldn't like it.

SHIRLEY: You can hardly read.

STEVEN: Never judge a book by its cover. Bet you get some funny sorts there though, eh?

IAN: Dead funny. There's some of the fellas, you can't tell what they are.

STEVEN: What d'you mean?

IAN: You know. Like if one came in here now and sat where I am, you wouldn't know – and before you knew it, he'd have his hand on your knee. (*He puts his hand on STEVEN's knee.*)

STEVEN: Get off.

IAN: Straight up.

STEVEN: Did you hear that?

SHIRLEY: Well you wouldn't have anything to worry about, you're ugly.

STEVEN: Lot of foreigners, too.

IAN: Yup.

STEVEN: It's like this place, with all the Paki shops and Indians opening up. Don't get us wrong, I'm not prejudiced, I just want 'em to go home that's all.

SHIRLEY: Where to?

STEVEN: Bradford. I wouldn't leave this place for all the tea in China – different for you though, you've got summat to go for – but Paul, he's just a drifter ain't he?

SHIRLEY: Whats' wrong with that?

STEVEN: He's got no purpose.

IAN: D'you want another pint?

STEVEN: Aye.

He finishes the rest of his pint in one and gives his glass to IAN.

The night is yet young.

The Gents. BILLY is smoking. NICKY and SHIRT enter.

NICKY: Lend us a fag mate.

BILLY: (*Looking up.*) It's me last one.

NICKY: That's alright, we only want one.

He takes a cigarette from BILLY.

Don't we Shirt?

SHIRT: (*Taking the cigarette from NICKY.*) Yeah, so it's lucky we bumped into you like this.

NICKY: Dead lucky.

BILLY: I was just off.

NICKY blocks BILLY's exit.

NICKY: Where to, church?

SHIRT: You shouldn't take the piss out of God.

BILLY: I never did.

NICKY: What's that you said about my sister?

BILLY: Nothin' – honest.

NICKY and SHIRT exit with BILLY. PAUL is on the phone again.

PAUL: Who's that?... I don't know you, who are you?... I want to speak to Jim... I can't... Because I'm not in London... it's long distance, I'm running out of money, it's urgent, I need him to... Shut up will you... A club... Tell him Paul rang, I'll ring him.

STEVEN, the worse for drink, is trying to pull SHIRLEY on the dance floor.

STEVEN: Come on Shirley.

SHIRLEY: I don't want to.

STEVEN: You like it when we dance.

SHIRLEY: No.

STEVEN: You'd prefer to dance with someone else?

SHIRLEY: Like who?

STEVEN: What about Paul?

SHIRLEY: Don't be ridiculous.

STEVEN: And you don't say anything else?

SHIRLEY: What else is there?

STEVEN: Like well done Steven, congratulations.

SHIRLEY: You're drunk.

STEVEN: So? I'm having a good time.

SHIRLEY: Well I'm not.

STEVEN: Look – sh, sh – he said, "Steven, the job's yours", that's it – I'm in the betting business, I've got a trade.

SHIRLEY: Don't spit in my face.

STEVEN: You stick with me girl, I'm gonna make a fuckin' fortune.

SHIRLEY: What does he want you to do this time, wash his car?

STEVEN: You don't like it because he's my friend.

SHIRLEY: I don't trust him.

STEVEN: It's favourites. Money for old rope, all you have to do is take their money – nobody wins.

SHIRLEY: I don't think Paul's coming back.

STEVEN: Disappointed?

SHIRLEY: Why should I be?

STEVEN: Listen, you'll like this – this fella comes in today, fifty quid like that, on the dogs – on the fucking dogs!

SHIRLEY: My glass is empty.

STEVEN: One minute he had fifty quid and the next it was in the Bookie's pocket.

SHIRLEY: I liked it better when you wanted to be an engineer.

STEVEN: He just gave it away, nobody forced him, nobody mugged him – fifty quid for two minutes' worth of dogs chasing round after a stuffed rabbit.

PAUL and IAN.

PAUL: Where's Billy?

IAN: Where have you been?

PAUL: Where's Billy?

IAN: He'll be alright. I'm going away tomorrow.

PAUL: Thanks.

IAN: Come with me. We could go now, pack our bags and just leave – piss on this place together.

PAUL: Where's Billy?

IAN: Come on.

PAUL: No.

IAN: Why not?

PAUL: 'Cos I don't want to.

IAN: Why?

PAUL: I'm off to look for Billy.

> *STEVEN and SHIRLEY.*

SHIRLEY: There's Paul.

STEVEN: Suppose you'd rather be talking to him.

SHIRLEY: No.

STEVEN: You fancy him.

SHIRLEY: No, I don't.

STEVEN: Yes, you do.

SHIRLEY: You're drunk.

STEVEN: You fancy him.

SHIRLEY: Alright. I fancy him – satisfied?

STEVEN: Yeah.

> *"My Girl" by the Temptations plays. MARY pulls PAUL on to the dance floor.*

PAUL: I can't dance.

MARY: What?

PAUL: I can't dance.

MARY: Of course you can.

PAUL: I feel stupid.

MARY: You don't look stupid. Just follow me, it's easy.

> *They dance. STEVEN comes up behind PAUL, taps him on the shoulder, PAUL turns his face and STEVEN punches it.*

STEVEN: I'm gonna kill you.

> *IAN pulls STEVEN away from PAUL.*

> The bastard slept with her, he slept with her.

IAN: Stay over there!

PAUL: You want a fight?

STEVEN: Yeah.

PAUL: Yeah?

STEVEN: Yeah!

IAN: (*Moving between them.*) Pack it in will you.

PAUL: I want to.

STEVEN: I'm not scared of him.

NICKY and SHIRT enter.

PAUL: Outside, now!

NICKY: What's goin' on here then?

IAN: Fuck off Tredwell.

STEVEN: I'm gonna kill the cunt.

NICKY and SHIRT drag IAN out of the way. They all fight. When it becomes obvious that PAUL has the upper hand on STEVEN, NICKY shoves STEVEN out of the way and pulls out his flick-knife on PAUL.

PAUL: Where's Billy?

NICKY: Being cared for.

SHIRT and IAN stop fighting. SHIRT holds IAN back.

STEVEN: I didn't agree to knives.

NICKY: He was beating the shit out of you.

PAUL: Why?

NICKY: Because I don't like your pretty face.

IAN: Kick him in the balls Steven.

STEVEN runs off. SHIRT, unsure of what to do, slackens his grip on IAN, IAN pushes past him and rushes at NICKY. NICKY turns and slashes wildly with his knife.

NICKY: Get back!

Unintentionally, the knife slashes across IAN's stomach. He stands still.

I said to keep back – I wasn't going to do anything, just scare him, I told you to keep back.

SHIRT runs off.

It was your own fault.

PAUL: Come on Nicky, do it.

NICKY: He just came at me.

PAUL: I'm waiting.

> *NICKY exits. PAUL rips off his shirt, and uses it as a bandage around IAN's stomach.*

Scene 20

IAN and PAUL.

IAN: Sit down will you.

PAUL: Watch it eh.

IAN: Go outside if you want one.

PAUL: I don't want to go outside, I want a fag. If there's any-where you need a fag it's hospital and they don't bloody let you.

IAN: It was your idea we come here, I'm alright.

PAUL: We're stayin' till someone sees you.

IAN: There's nothing wrong.

PAUL: You're bleeding, look at me shirt.

IAN: I didn't ask you to wrap it round me – it just looks worse than it is that's all.

PAUL: What's taking them so long, I don't see what the hold-up is.

IAN: Just have a fag will you.

PAUL: I can't. You'll need stitches.

IAN: Give over, it's just a scratch.

PAUL: D'you fancy a drink?

IAN: I'm still going away tomorrow – why don't you come with us?

PAUL: I've already said. Well, do you?

IAN: What.

PAUL: Want a drink.

IAN: No.

PAUL: You can't anyway, they might have to give you an
  anaesthetic.

IAN: So why ask.

PAUL: 'Cos I'm looking after you.

IAN: You have a drink if you want one.

PAUL: I don't.

IAN: I'm not going back to college.

PAUL: You'll go back.

IAN: I've decided.

PAUL: What you gonna do instead?

IAN: I dunno.

PAUL: You'll go back.

IAN: What are you gonna do? Who was that you were on the
  phone to?

PAUL: A friend, alright.

IAN: In London – the one that you shagged?

PAUL: Who says I shagged anyone in London?

IAN: Billy.

PAUL: Wish they'd hurry up and see you.

IAN: Why won't you tell me?

PAUL: I've told thee, there's nothing to tell. She's older then
  me... She helped us out, said I could stay at her house for
  a while, so I did and we got a bit friendly. So she writes to
  me, I ring her up now and again, that's all there is.

IAN: Why did you leave?

PAUL: Because I had to, to clear me 'ead and now you're
  doin' it in again.

IAN: She married?

PAUL: I don't see what the hold-up is.

IAN: Go home if you want.

PAUL: I don't.

IAN: Have you fucked Shirley?

PAUL: What if I have, what's it to you.

IAN: Nothing.

PAUL: I fuck who I like.

IAN: Oh aye?

PAUL: Piss off.

IAN: Whose girlfriend haven't you tried to fuck?

PAUL: You what.

IAN: What about Rosemary Tredwell.

PAUL: I never touched her.

IAN: You never learn do you, you can't just go round screwing everyone's girlfriend.

PAUL: Why not?

IAN: Because you can't, you hear?

PAUL: Yeah, yeah.

IAN: What's the matter with you eh, what's the matter.

PAUL: Nothing, alright.

IAN: If you want a girlfriend get one.

PAUL: I don't.

IAN: What do you want?

PAUL: You know don't you.

IAN: What, what do I know?

PAUL: You've known all along.

IAN: Known what?

PAUL: So why d'you want me to come away?

IAN: I just think we could have a bit of fun, you know. You can always go to London after, maybe I'll come with you. I don't see what the problem is.

PAUL: Nothing, there's no problem – I'll think about it, alright, now stop goin' on.

IAN: Have a fag.

PAUL: I can't.

IAN: Go on.

PAUL: No.

IAN: Have a fag.

PAUL: I'll go outside.

Scene 21

PAUL is filling a bag with his belongings. He tries to fit a pair of baseball shoes in, then leaves them out. BILLY enters, arm in a sling.

BILLY: Where are you going?

PAUL: London.

BILLY: I'm not coming then?

PAUL: No. You can come and visit when I get settled in.

BILLY: Yeah. D'you know where yet?

PAUL: No – wait till I get there.

BILLY: You won't have any problems though.

PAUL: Shouldn't think so. You'll be alright. How's the arm?

BILLY: You don't have to go you know – I don't mind sleeping on the couch all the time – it's more comfortable than the bed. There won't be any trains yet.

PAUL: I'm not takin' train.

BILLY: How you goin' then? I've got money.

PAUL: I don't want your money.

BILLY hands PAUL a five pound note.

BILLY: Go on – for a cuppa tea like.

PAUL: I can't stay, I've got to go, right.

BILLY: It'll be alright for me to come and visit then.

PAUL: Yeah, I've already said 'aven't I – why, don't you want to come anymore?

BILLY: No – if it doesn't work out you can always come back.

PAUL: Yeah.

BILLY: I'm on days next week.

PAUL throws BILLY the baseball boots.

PAUL: A present – they won't fit in me bag.

BILLY: They're too big.

PAUL: Put some extra socks on then.

BILLY: Hang on – you've forgot summat.

BILLY gives PAUL a letter, opened.

PAUL: Have you read it?

BILLY: Yeah.

PAUL: D'you read all my letters?

BILLY: No – just the ones from London, I steam them open. They're interesting.

PAUL: I don't open yours do I?

BILLY: I don't get any.

PAUL: You read it?

BILLY: An' if I did I wouldn't mind.

PAUL: You read it?

BILLY: That who you stay with in London is it?

PAUL: Yeah.

BILLY: You sure he won't mind me coming?

PAUL: Yeah.

BILLY: Sounds alright then.

PAUL: Yeah.

BILLY: It doesn't bother me you know.

PAUL: What doesn't bother you?

BILLY: I'm just saying – it doesn't bother me. How did you meet him?

PAUL: In a pub.

BILLY: That's nice.

PAUL: I didn't have any money.

BILLY: Buy you a drink did he?

PAUL: Yeah. We went back to his place and he didn't make me do anything, we just slept in the same bed. It's like what he wants most is the company, like he just enjoys having me there. We have a laugh, he takes me places and I feel alright, he makes me feel alright. He never makes me do anything I don't want, but I don't mind, as long as we don't do it too often. I've told him I'm not queer, says he knows, says he understands. He always makes sure I'm alright – for money, you know.

BILLY: What's his name? I can never make out his signature.

PAUL: Jim.

They both laugh.

BILLY: Why did you leave?

PAUL: I was beginning to like him.

BILLY: So why are you going back?

PAUL: I don't know that I am – wait and see what happens when I get there.

Scene 22

The café.

SHIRLEY: Have you ever been to Eastbourne?

MARY: No.

SHIRLEY: Me neither.

MARY: Cold and dead like this place is it?

SHIRLEY: I don't know. Funny how it all just drops off isn't it – like there's no in-between, either there's people or there isn't.

MARY: I hate the winter.

SHIRLEY: It's only September.

MARY: It's cold.

Pause.

SHIRLEY: I might be going to Eastbourne soon.

MARY: When?

SHIRLEY: It's not definite – they're opening this new hotel and they want me down there on the desk.

MARY: Is there no-one in Eastbourne they can get?

SHIRLEY: It's not definite. It's just they need someone with a bit of personality and life. I'd have me own room, with *en suite* shower and bathroom.

MARY: Don't need any chambermaids do they?

SHIRLEY: It's called The Wish Tower, four star.

MARY: Some people have all the luck.

SHIRLEY: At least you've got a fella.

MARY: So could you if you wanted.

SHIRLEY: Men aren't everything you know Mary.

MARY: I know.

Pause.

Where is Eastbourne?

SHIRLEY: Somewhere near London I think. Anyroad, it wouldn't be for long, six months at the most.

MARY: Well I might not be here when you get back.

SHIRLEY: Where you going?

MARY: I don't know.

SHIRLEY: I can always ring you.

MARY: We're not married you know. (*She pauses.*) Anything could happen in six months – I might enter a competition and win a ticket round the world, or I might just get on a plane and go far away to some exotic place.

SHIRLEY: Well if you do, send us a postcard.

STEVEN and NICKY enter.

That's it, I'm going.

MARY: Sit down will you.

STEVEN: Hello Shirley, how you keeping?

SHIRLEY: Fine.

STEVEN: Haven't seen you for a while.

SHIRLEY: No, not since yesterday – I saw you following me.

STEVEN: Anyone sitting there?

SHIRLEY: Yes.

NICKY: Don't waste your breath, she's not worth the effort.

MARY: Who let you out your cage?

NICKY: G'ez a coffee Steve.

SHIRLEY: How much does he pay you?

NICKY: And a cheese'n'onion butty while you're up there.

STEVEN exits. NICKY sits at another table.

SHIRLEY: I can't go anywhere without him following me;
even when I'm having a pee I keep expectin' him to poke
his head round the door. Don't know why he's hanging
round with Nicky Tredwell, thought he had more sense.
And as for his hair it's just bloody daft, what's he want to
go and stick all that glue on it for?

MARY: Why don't you go and ask him?

SHIRLEY: I'm not interested.

BILLY enters, arm out of sling.

MARY: Shirley's going to Eastbourne.

BILLY: Oh aye, what for?

SHIRLEY: It's not decided.

*STEVEN enters with coffee and a sandwich. SHIRLEY goes to leave
and nearly bumps into STEVEN.*

Bloody hell Steven.

SHIRLEY exits.

BILLY: Got a card from Paul this morning. Sounds alright.
Didn't say much mind, just hello.

MARY: Is he still with that girl?

BILLY: Dunno, didn't say.

STEVEN: Jesus, I haven't had a poke in weeks, if I don't have one soon I'll go barmy.

NICKY: What d'you think your right hand's for?

STEVEN: It's worn out. I keep getting these aches –

NICKY: It's got mustard on it.

STEVEN: Yeah, I like mustard.

NICKY: I can't eat that – go and get us another.

STEVEN: I haven't got any money.

BILLY: We could go to the pictures.

MARY: There's nothing on.

BILLY: What about my place then? Get some cans in and watch the telly.

    SHIRLEY enters.

SHIRLEY: Here, they're shutting this place down at the end of the week.

MARY: Won't bother you will it, you'll be in Eastbourne – expect things stay open longer down there.

BILLY: And it's warmer.

MARY: Shut up Billy.

BILLY: Well it is, it's nearer the Equator.

NICKY: (*Shouting.*) How's the arm Billy?

BILLY: Yeah, great.

MARY: Don't talk to him.

NICKY: It's out the sling then.

BILLY: Yeah.

MARY: God you're soft.

SHIRLEY: Don't say that – for any successful relationship to work, each partner must treat the other with mutual respect.

MARY: I'm going out with him, not going into business with him.

SHIRLEY: That's why mine and Steven's relationship didn't work – I didn't respect him and all he could see me as was something to worship, a love goddess.

MARY: Bloody hell, where d'you get that from?

NICKY comes over and offers his hand to BILLY.

NICKY: No hard feelings like?

BILLY: I won't if you don't mind, it's still a bit sore.

NICKY: Aye. We just got a bit carried away that's all. Nothing personal.

BILLY: Yeah.

Pause.

NICKY: Which one of them are you shagging then?

SHIRLEY: Both of us.

MARY: Yeah both of us and at the same time.

SHIRLEY and MARY exit.

BILLY: I'd best be off. See you around then.

NICKY: Expect so.

BILLY: Cheers Steve.

STEVEN: Cheers.

BILLY exits.

What d'you go and ask a daft question like that for?

NICKY: Felt like it.

Pause.

STEVEN: You don't think he is do you? I've never done it with two in a bed.

NICKY: You can have me sandwich if you want.

STEVEN: Yeah, ta.

STEVEN eats the sandwich. NICKY reads the paper. Silence.

THE END